# CITY
# ON
# FIRE

# September 11
# 23 Elul 5761

*Background, Stories, and Torah Insights*

Compiled and Edited by
**Sorah Shapiro**

TARGUM/FELDHEIM

First published 2002
Copyright © 2002 by Sorah Shapiro
ISBN 1-56871-269-3

*Published by:*
Targum Press, Inc.
22700 W. Eleven Mile Rd.
Southfield, MI 48034
E-mail: targum@netvision.net.il
Fax: 888-298-9992
www.targum.com

*Distributed by:*
Feldheim Publishers
202 Airport Executive Park
Nanuet, NY 10954

*Printed in Israel*

*Photocredits:*
*Cover: AP/Wide World Photos*
*Inside: Nosson Josephy*
*Picture of men crossing bridge: Steve Solomonson*

This book is dedicated
to the memory of

my mother

רחל לאה בת ר׳ שלמה הלוי ע״ה

and my father

חיים מיכל בן ר׳ יעקב ע״ה

This book is dedicated

to all those

who lost their lives

or their loved ones

on that day.

# Contents

## IN MEMORIAM

# Acknowledgments

This book would never have come to be if not for the literary contributions of the individuals and organizations named throughout its pages and their spouses and representatives. No words can adequately express my appreciation to each and every one of you for having enhanced the work and enriching us with your wisdom.

Heartfelt thanks also to Agudath Israel, Henry Alper, Tzvi Bobker, Chofetz Chaim Heritage Foundation, Rabbi Henoch Cohen, Jacque Friedman, Rabbi David Grossman, Rabbi Yaakov Yitzchok and Esther Herzka, Rebbetzin Rochel Kelemer, M. L., A. Eliyahu Mallenbaum, Hindy Moskowitz, Rabbi Yaakov Neiman, Chaim Pabak, the Rand family, Rabbi Yehuda Rokovsky, Rabbi Eliahu Rominek, Rabbi A. J. Rosenberg, Bernard Rothman, Rabbi Arye Schechter, Ari Simpson, Tamar, Rabbi Eli Teitelbaum, Moishe Weintraub, Nachman Wolfson, Rabbi Nisson Wolpin, and countless others who lent a hand or an ear.

A special debt of gratitude to Rabbi Moshe Dombey, Miriam Zakon, Suri Brand, D. Liff, and the entire staff of Targum Press for a smooth sail to publication and their professionalism.

To those I have inadvertently omitted or failed to acknowledge, my deepest *hakaras hatov* for everything.

To my readers: May we meet on happier occasions.

Above all, I thank and praise the *Borei olam* for the opportunity to put to paper an event that will be permanently imprinted in memory.

Sorah Shapiro
Brooklyn, New York
Adar 5762

# Introduction

$A$nd it came to pass that on Tuesday, September 11, 2001, which was the twenty-third day of Elul, in the year 5761, exactly one week before Rosh HaShanah, three hijacked planes crashed into major U.S. landmarks, destroying New York's mighty Twin Towers and causing the Pentagon in Washington to be engulfed in flames.

Saudi-born Islamic militant and millionaire Osama bin Laden was cited as the source of the unprecedented terrorist attack on key symbols of U.S. military and financial power. The guerilla leader had also been blamed for the 1998 bombings of the U.S. embassies in Kenya and Tanzania, in which 224 people died, last year's bombing of a U.S. Navy ship in Yemen, and foiled plots in the United States and Jordan at the turn of the millennium.

The assault, the most pernicious on the U.S. mainland in modern history, plunged the country into fear and panic, paralyzing communication, forcing the evacuation of key buildings, closing markets, schools, and businesses. Sirens shrieked as the terrified masses scuttled through the streets seeking safety.

The nightmare began at around 9 A.M. in New York, when the first plane plowed into the north tower of New York's World Trade Center, as thousands of workers thronged into the building to begin their workday. Within two hours the whole building, in which tens of thousands of employees and visitors were usually present, collapsed on itself in a huge cloud of smoke and fire. The second plane plowed into the second of the Twin Towers, which exploded in a fireball and caved in about an hour after the first.

Soon afterward a third plane crashed into the Pentagon in Washington, throwing people off their feet inside the building and setting off a massive fire.

Another flight crashed just outside of Pittsburgh.

There were thousands of casualties.

That is what happened. Theories as to why it happened and how it happened are as numerous and divergent as the pieces of a jigsaw puzzle. The architect, the economist, the historian, the politician, the armchair philosopher, each sees it from his vantage point. The *rabbanim* and the observant Jew, of course, view it from a Torah perspective. Though no mortal man can understand the Creator's ways, we know that nothing in this world can happen unless it is His will.

We bring you here a mass of information and viewpoints, which prove that "*tachlis hayedia shelo neida* – the end result of knowledge is the knowledge that we know nothing." For the believer, there are no questions; for the nonbeliever, no answers.

Sorah Shapiro
Brooklyn, New York
Adar 5762

# CHAPTER ONE

# Background: The Twin Towers

## GENERAL INFORMATION

*By Sorah Shapiro*

*Height*: 1,368 feet and 1,362 feet (417 meters and 415 meters)

*Owners*: Port Authority of New York and New Jersey

*Leased to*: Silverstein Properties (Larry Silverstein)

*Architect*: Minoru Yamasaki, Emery Roth and Sons Consulting

*Engineers*: John Skilling and Leslie Robertson (Worthington, Skilling, Helle, and Jackson)

*Builder*: Tishman Realty

*Construction supervisor*: Hyman Brown

*Groundbreaking*: August 5, 1966

*Opened*: 1970–73; ribbon cutting, April 4, 1973

*Destroyed*: Terrorist attack, September 11, 2001

The Twin Towers were the world's tallest buildings for a short time, taking the title from the Empire State Building, until it was topped by the Sears Tower in Chicago.

Minoru Yamasaki, who was selected over a dozen other American architects, worked in collaboration with his engineers, John Skilling and Les Robertson, to devise a structure of unparalleled height, patterned after the IBM Building in Seattle. After studying more than one hundred schemes in model form, he decided on a two-tower construction of 9 million square feet of office space. One tower would have been impractical in size and structure, and multiple towers would resemble a housing project. Two towers presented a reasonable compromise that would allow ample office space, a forty-five-mile view in every direction, and a practical structural system. The Twin Towers, with 110 floors rising 1,360 feet, would be the world's tallest.

He devised an ingenious structural model: a strong "hollow tube" of closely spaced steel columns with floor trusses extending across to a central core. The 208-foot-wide exterior was, in effect, a prefabricated steel lattice, with columns on thirty-nine-inch centers to withstand wind and other toppling forces; the central core would take only the gravity loads of the building.

The building's interior had no columns. There was about forty thousand square feet of office space on each of the upper floors. The floor was made of prefabricated trussed steel, thirty-three inches in depth, covering the full sixty feet to the core, which served as a barrier against wind-load pressures. The columns, coated with a silver-colored aluminum alloy, were 18.75 inches wide and set only 22 inches apart, making

the towers appear windowless from afar.

Equally unique were its core and elevator system. The Twin Towers were the first skyscrapers to be constructed without masonry. To avoid the contingency of buckling, as might occur with conventional elevator shafts, engineers designed a drywall system anchored to the reinforced steel core. To service 110 stories, half the space of the lower stories would have had to be used for shafts, but Otis Elevators developed an express and local system, whereby passengers would change at "sky lobbies" on the forty-fourth and seventy-eighth floors, reducing the number of shafts by half.

## WHO OWNS THE TWIN TOWERS?

*By Sorah Shapiro*

*The Twin Towers are owned and managed by the Port Authority of New York and New Jersey, a joint venture, which also owns and manages JFK Airport, Newark Airport, and La Guardia Airport.*

Only ten days before the attack, the Port Authority gave Larry Silverstein, a private real-estate developer, a ninety-nine-year lease to the towers. He paid $616 million down and agreed to pay $3 billion in lease payments over the next ninety-nine years in return for rights to manage and rent out the towers.

His partner, Westfield America Inc., owns the ninety-nine-year lease for the 425,000-square-foot retail portion. Frank Lowy, chairman and founder of Westfield Holdings, the manager of Westfield America Trust, which owns 57 percent of

Westfield America Inc., is the second wealthiest man in Australia, the United States, the United Kingdom, and New Zealand and was ranked by Forbes as the 209th wealthiest man in the world. He is a renowned philanthropist in Sydney and in Israel. Lowy said his corporation was covered against terrorist attacks and earnings would not suffer.

## WORLD TRADE CENTER BECAME JEWEL OF MANHATTAN'S DOWNTOWN

*By Mark Evans, The Associated Press*
*(The Daily Camera, September 12, 2001)*
*Reprinted with permission*

*NEW YORK – In a city full of famous buildings, the Twin Towers of the World Trade Center outdid them all – massive glass-and-steel sculptures that appeared to float above the tip of lower Manhattan.*

At 110 floors each, the boxlike pillars looked simple in form, but they were sturdy architectural marvels that provided a home for 1,200 businesses, many of them involved in international trade.

First imagined in the early 1960s as part of an urban renewal project, the first buildings in the $1.2 billion, 16-acre complex opened in 1970.

The Twin Towers were completed in 1976, immense in every detail – forty-three thousand windows, ninety-nine elevators, 1,350 feet tall – and designed to be a critical hub for international trade. At the time, they were the tallest buildings in the world; until Tuesday, they remained the tallest in New York.

The buildings were designed to be especially sturdy, using

load-bearing steel walls rather than the steel-cage construction typical of modern skyscrapers.

By the time the final building of the seven-building complex was completed in 1988, the center had lured scores of businesses, including commodity exchanges, major investment firms, banks, law firms, and a hotel.

The center was fully rented out when the towers collapsed Tuesday. Roughly fifty thousand people worked in the towers; the complex, which included an observation deck and a number of other tourist attractions, drew an additional ninety thousand visitors each day, according to the Port Authority of New York and New Jersey, which runs the complex.

While it thrived as an international business hub, it also had become a clear target for terrorists.

On February 23, 1993, bombs exploded in a parking garage beneath the center, killing six people and injuring one thousand. Six Islamic militants were convicted in the bombing and sentenced to life behind bars.

FBI evidence in that case included documents from one conspirator, who wrote that the bombing was meant to demoralize the enemy by "blowing up the towers that constitute the pillars of their civilization."

Tuesday's tragedy clearly had that effect on Lewis Eisenberg, chairman of the Port Authority of New York and New Jersey, who said he was "devastated beyond belief."

"I mean, in many respects this is significantly worse than Pearl Harbor, and we don't know who the enemy is. As Americans we will pull together and do what's right."

He said he was stunned: "I just saw my two towers fall."

# CHAPTER TWO

# Background: The Attack and the Attackers

## WORLD TRADE CENTER COLLAPSES
### Washington Hit by Apparently Coordinated Attack

*By Jerry Schwartz, The Associated Press*
*(The Daily Camera, September 12, 2001)*
*Reprinted with permission*

*NEW YORK – Mounting an audacious attack against the United States, terrorists crashed two hijacked airliners into the World Trade Center and brought down the twin 110-story towers Tuesday morning. A jetliner also slammed into the Pentagon as the seat of government itself came under attack.*

Hundreds were apparently killed aboard the jets, and untold numbers were feared dead in the rubble. Thousands were injured in New York alone.

A fourth jetliner, also apparently hijacked, crashed in Pennsylvania.

President Bush ordered a full-scale investigation to "hunt down the folks who committed this act."

Authorities were still trying to evacuate those who work in the Twin Towers when the glass-and-steel skyscrapers came down in a thunderous roar within about ninety minutes after the attacks, which took place eighteen minutes apart around 9 A.M. Many people were feared trapped. About fifty thousand people work at the Trade Center, and tens of thousands of others visit each day.

Officials said the Trade Center apparently was hit by two planes carrying a total of 157 people: United Airlines Flight 175, a Boeing 767 bound from Boston to Los Angeles with sixty-five people on board, and American Airlines Flight 11, a Los Angeles-bound jet hijacked after takeoff from Boston with ninety-two people aboard.

Law enforcement officials, speaking on condition of anonymity, said the Pentagon was hit by American Flight 77, which was seized while carrying sixty-four people from Washington to Los Angeles.

And in Pennsylvania, United Flight 93, a Boeing 757 en route from Newark, New Jersey, to San Francisco, crashed about eighty miles southeast of Pittsburgh with forty-five people aboard. A Virginia congressman, Representative James Moran, said the intended target of that plane was apparently Camp David, the presidential retreat in Maryland, eight-five miles away.

Altogether, the four planes carried 266 people. There was no word on any survivors.

At the Trade Center, people on fire leaped from the windows to certain death.... Some jumped from as high as the eightieth floor as the planes exploded into fireballs. People on the ground screamed and dived for cover as debris from the 1,350-foot towers rained down. Dazed office workers covered in gray ash wandered around like ghosts, weeping, trying to make sense of what happened.

Donald Burns, thirty-four, who had been at a meeting on the eighty-second floor, saw four severely burned people on the stairwell. "I tried to help them, but they didn't want anyone to touch them. The fire had melted their skin. Their clothes were tattered," he said.

"People were screaming, falling, and jumping out of the windows," from high in the sky, said Jennifer Brickhouse, thirty-four, of Union, New Jersey, who was going up the escalator into the World Trade Center.

Within the hour after the attack in New York, the Pentagon took a direct, devastating hit from a plane. The fiery crash collapsed one side of the five-sided structure.

Speculation about the attack quickly focused on terrorist fugitive Osama bin Laden.

"No one has been ruled out, but our initial feeling is that this is the work of bin Laden," said a high-ranking federal law enforcement official who spoke on condition of anonymity. "He is top of our list at this point."

"This is perhaps the most audacious terrorist attack that's ever taken place in the world," said Chris Yates, an aviation expert at Jane's Transport in London. "It takes a logistics operation from the terror group involved that is second to none.

Only a very small handful of terror groups is on that list.... I would name at the top of the list Osama bin Laden."

The president put the military on its highest level of alert. Authorities in Washington immediately called out troops, including an infantry regiment, and the Navy sent aircraft carriers and guided missile destroyers to New York and Washington.

The White House, the Pentagon, and the Capitol were evacuated along with other federal buildings in Washington and New York. The president was taken to Offutt Air Force Base in Nebraska, headquarters for the Strategic Air Command, the nation's nuclear strike force, the White House said. Later, he headed back to Washington.

The U.S. and Canadian borders were sealed, security was tightened at naval installations and other strategic points, and all commercial air traffic across the country was halted until at least noon on Wednesday.

"This is the second Pearl Harbor. I don't think that I overstate it," said Senator Chuck Hagel, R-Neb. The December 7, 1941, Japanese attack on Pearl Harbor killed nearly 2,400 people and drew the United States into World War II.

Senator John McCain, R-Ariz., said, "These attacks clearly constitute an act of war."

In June, a U.S. judge had set Wednesday as the sentencing date for a bin Laden associate for his role in the 1998 bombing of a U.S. Embassy in Tanzania that killed 213 people. The sentencing had been set for the federal courthouse near the World Trade Center. But the sentencing had been postponed some time ago without being rescheduled.

Afghanistan's hard-line Taliban rulers condemned the attacks and rejected suggestions that bin Laden was behind them, saying he does not have the means to carry out such well-orchestrated attacks. Bin Laden has been given asylum in Afghanistan.

Abdel-Bari Atwan, editor of the *Al-Quds al-Arabi* newspaper, said he received a warning from Islamic fundamentalists close to bin Laden, but did not take the threat seriously. "They said it would be a huge and unprecedented attack, but they did not specify," Atwan said in a telephone interview in London.

In the West Bank city of Nablus, thousands of Palestinians celebrated the attacks, chanting, "God is great," and handing out candy.

In New York, the downtown area was cordoned off, and a rescue effort was under way. Hundreds of volunteers and medical workers converged on triage centers, offering help and blood. Paramedics waiting to be sent into the rubble were told that "once the smoke clears, it's going to be massive bodies," said Brian Stark, a former Navy paramedic who volunteered to help.

He said the paramedics had been told that hundreds of police and firefighters were missing from the ranks of those sent in to respond to the first crash.

Mayor Rudolph Giuliani said 2,100 people were injured — 1,500 "walking wounded" who were taken to New Jersey, and 600 others who were taken to area hospitals, 150 of them in critical condition. It could take weeks to dig through the rubble for victims.

"I have a sense it's a horrendous number of lives lost,"

Giuliani said. "Right now we have to focus on saving as many lives as possible."

By evening, huge clouds of smoke still billowed from the ruins, obscuring much of the skyline. Also, fire raged at an adjoining forty-seven-story part of the World Trade Center complex, and the evacuated building was in danger of collapse, the Fire Department said.

The two planes blasted fiery, gaping holes in the upper floors of one of New York's most famous landmarks and rained debris on the streets. About an hour later, the southern tower collapsed with a roar and a huge cloud of smoke; the other tower fell about a half-hour after that, covering lower Manhattan in heaps of gray rubble and broken glass.

On the street, a crowd mobbed a man at a pay phone, screaming at him to get off the phone so that they could call relatives. Dust and dirt flew everywhere. Ash was two to three inches deep in places.

John Axisa, who was getting off a commuter train to the World Trade Center, said he saw "bodies falling out" of the building. He said he ran outside and watched people jump out of the first building. Then there was a second explosion, and he felt heat on the back of his neck.

David Reck was handing out literature for a candidate for public advocate a few blocks away when he saw a jet come in "very low, and then it made a slight twist and dove into the building."

People ran down the stairs in panic and fled the building. Thousands of pieces of what appeared to be office paper drifted over Brooklyn, about three miles away.

Several subway lines were immediately shut down. Trading on Wall Street was suspended. New York's mayoral primary election Tuesday was postponed. All bridges and tunnels into Manhattan were closed.

The death toll on the crashed planes alone could surpass that of the Oklahoma City bombing on April 19, 1995, which claimed 168 lives in what was the deadliest act of terrorism on U.S. soil.

"Today we've had a national tragedy," Bush said in Sarasota, Florida. "Two airplanes have crashed into the World Trade Center in an apparent terrorist attack on our country." He said he would be returning immediately to Washington.

Evacuations were ordered at the United Nations in New York and at the Sears Tower in Chicago. Los Angeles mobilized its anti-terrorism division. Walt Disney World in Orlando, Florida, was evacuated, and Hoover Dam on the Arizona-Nevada line was closed to visitors.

Terrorists blew up a truck bomb in the basement of the World Trade Center in February 1993, killing six people and injuring more than one thousand others.

"It's just sick. It just shows how vulnerable we really are," Keith Meyers, thirty-nine, said in Columbus, Ohio. "It kind of makes you want to go home and spend time with your family. It puts everything in perspective," Meyers said. He said he called to check in with his wife. They have two young children.

In 1945, an Army Air Corps B-25, a twin-engine bomber, crashed into the seventy-ninth floor of the Empire State Building in dense fog.

In Florida, Bush was reading to children in a classroom at 9:05 A.M. when his chief of staff, Andrew Card, whispered into his ear. The president briefly turned somber before he resumed reading. He addressed the tragedy about a half-hour later.

Before the crash in Pennsylvania, an emergency dispatcher in Westmoreland County, Pennsylvania, received a cell phone call at 9:58 A.M. from a man who said he was a passenger locked in the bathroom of United Flight 93, said dispatch supervisor Glenn Cramer.

"We are being hijacked! We are being hijacked!" Cramer quoted the man as saying. The man told dispatchers the plane "was going down." He heard some sort of explosion and saw white smoke coming from the plane, and we lost contact with him, Cramer said.

## TERROR EXPERTS POINT FINGER AT BIN LADEN

*Scripps Howard News Service*
*(The Daily Camera, September 12, 2001)*
*Reprinted with permission*

*By early afternoon Tuesday, after four airliners were hijacked and crashed into the World Trade Center towers, the Pentagon and Pennsylvania woods, national security experts were all but convinced that the well-planned and executed terrorism carried the signature of the al Qaeda group and, most likely, its titular leader, Osama bin Laden.*

"I know of no other group that could have done this," said Jerrold Post, a George Washington University professor who testified at the recent trial of al Qaeda members for their roles in the 1993 bombing of the World Trade Center.

Post and others said the U.S. attacks essentially were airplane versions of the suicide truck- and boat-bomb attacks that bin Laden–related Islamic extremists conducted in past years against the World Trade Center, a U.S. Air Force highrise in Saudi Arabia, U.S. embassies in Kenya and Tanzania, and the Navy warship USS *Cole* in a Yemeni port.

They said none other of the twenty-nine terrorist organizations identified this year by the State Department as potential global threats has the experience, coordination skills, and logistical ability to orchestrate the attacks that effectively paralyzed the nation's capital and brought the rest of the nation to a frightened halt.

Al Qaeda is a loosely linked umbrella organization that connects anti-American and anti-Israeli activists affiliated with a host of long-established Middle East terror groups, including Hizbullah, Islamic Jihad, the Armed Islamic Group, and others.

The coalition also includes small cells of followers that U.S. officials have identified in Iraq, Sudan, Pakistan, Jordan, England, Indonesia, Lebanon, Bosnia, France, Saudi Arabia, New York, Santa Clara, California, and the Dallas–Fort Worth area.

Bin Laden, the son of a Saudi magnate who has been linked to more than a decade of anti-American terror, functions as the spiritual and inspirational leader of those committed to jihad, or religious war, against America and Israel. Topping the FBI's most-wanted list for five years with a $5 million bounty for his arrest, bin Laden is believed to be based in Afghanistan, where the Islamic extremist Taliban government has protected him in the past.

Taliban officials Tuesday denied any connection with the airplane bomb attacks in Washington, Pennsylvania, and New York.

Counterterrorism experts say a host of signs point toward al Qaeda. The group has vowed retaliation since the May convictions of four of its allegedly affiliated operatives in New York for their roles in the 1998 embassy bombings in Africa, declaring a new level for its holy war against America and Israel.

That rage has only intensified as the Israeli-Palestinian situation has deteriorated into a bloody slow-motion war. The experts said the timing of Tuesday's attacks − coming two days before the eighth anniversary of the Israel-Palestinian peace pact that was sealed at the White House − could carry significance. They noted, too, that sentencing for the embassy bombers in New York was scheduled for Wednesday.

CIA and FBI counterterrorism experts say the far-flung cells and groups coordinate through al Qaeda's Shura Council, a kind of board of directors that meets on a regular basis in Afghanistan.

"Most of them have maintained close relationships with each other since the end of the war in Afghanistan against the Soviets [in the 1980s]. They know each other well and work together efficiently," Washington terrorist expert Daniel Pipes recently wrote.

The workings of al Qaeda came into public focus this year during the embassy bombing trial. Between terror attacks, network members operate under the cover of everyday businesses and Islamic and other charity groups. For example, the Qatar Charitable Society, which has solicited funds in the United States, has served as a conduit for raising and transferring funds, terrorism experts say.

The network has also been successful in procuring such items as night-vision goggles, cell phones, and construction equipment to chemicals and bomb-making material and efficiently distributing it to whichever cell needs it.

And although bin Laden is their figurehead, the members carry such an ideological zeal that even his capture or killing would little hamper their mission to defeat all "enemies" of Islam. When operations in one area are disrupted, the rest of the network marches on.

"Islamism is the glue that keeps these groups together and fired up," Pipes said.

## THE TALIBAN: SHELTERING TERROR

*By Tony Karon (2002 Time, Inc.)*
*Reprinted with permission*

*Who are the Taliban and why are they sheltering Osama bin Laden?*

The Taliban, who overran most of Afghanistan in 1996, are a militia driven by an extremely harsh, medieval interpretation of Sunni Islam. Backed by Pakistan and funded by Saudi Arabia, they promised to put an end to the factional warfare that had claimed thousands of lives in the years following the defeat of the country's Soviet puppet government in 1991. The Taliban imposed an extremely repressive, sectarian Islamic regime on the Afghan people, barring women from work and education and even killing Shiite Muslims of the Hazari minority.

Bin Laden had been a hero of the jihad against the Soviet occupiers, and the Taliban welcomed him back to Afghanistan in 1996 after his expulsion from the Sudan. Bin Laden has reportedly cemented his ties to the Taliban leadership through his daughter's marriage to its leader, Mullah Omar. But, more importantly, his Arab Afghan fighters have played a leading role in the Taliban's ongoing military campaign against its opponents. The Taliban's elite brigade were trained in bin Laden's camps and are believed to be loyal to the Saudi terrorist's al Qaeda movement.

*Is the Taliban the recognized government of Afghanistan?
Do they have domestic opposition?*

Only Pakistan, Saudi Arabia, and the United Arab Emirates recognize the Taliban as Afghanistan's government, and international recognition as a legitimate government remains the movement's most important foreign policy objective. The country's seat at the United Nations is still held by representatives of the government overthrown by the Taliban in 1996, to which the opposition Northern Alliance remains loyal.

The Northern Alliance is a loose anti-Taliban coalition that includes remnants of the former Soviet-backed regime and a number of ethnic, minority-based groups fiercely opposed to the Taliban's harsh rule — and also to the principle of being ruled by a government composed only of ethnic Pashtuns.

The key component of these forces are the ethnic Tajiks, who control the strategically important Pansjir Valley. The Taliban have failed to dislodge them despite launching massive annual offensives — but they did strike a body blow last week by assassinating the Northern Alliance's key military leader, Ahmed Shah Masood, the "Lion of the Pansjir." The Northern Alliance forces only control 5 percent of the country, but the Taliban's harsh regime has provoked growing resentment, even among Afghans who initially welcomed their takeover.

*Is it possible that the Taliban would hand over bin Laden for trial?*

It's unlikely, but it's not impossible. The Taliban's priorities are quite different from bin Laden's. They want to build and consolidate an Islamic state in Afghanistan; he's waging a global jihad. And right now those priorities are somewhat in conflict, because, as Pakistan has tried to warn its erstwhile protegés, standing with bin Laden now will spark a confrontation that could see the Taliban overthrown. But the Taliban has become so dependent on bin Laden's own forces and men loyal to him that they may struggle to rationalize giving him up without facing internal disintegration. They're likely to play for time and try and fudge the issue, and it wouldn't be surprising to hear Taliban spokesmen in the very near future proclaiming that bin Laden has left Afghanistan, regardless of his actual whereabouts.

> *How have Afghanistan's neighbors responded to the Taliban?*

Pakistan has been more than a friend to the Taliban — in many ways it has been mentor and tutor, too, and even, according to opposition groups, an active participant in its rise to power. In geopolitical terms, Pakistan needs to dominate Afghanistan to offset the discomfort of being wedged between hostile neighbors India and (to a lesser, but not insignificant extent) Iran — and the Taliban were to have been their vehicle. But the bin Laden terror campaign has put Pakistan in a tight spot, where its all-important relations with the West are now dependent on standing against its Afghan progeny, a decision that raises considerable domestic difficulty for Pakistan's leaders.

China shares a small border with Afghanistan and has been generally supportive of the U.S. call for action against terrorism. Bin Laden's group has trained Islamists fighting for secession in western China, and Beijing would be happy to see an end to the regime in Afghanistan that allows terrorist training camps to be maintained there. The Chinese have moved troops to the border recently, but are unlikely to support any direct U.S. military intervention in their neighborhood, much less allow their own territory to be used.

Beijing's importance may lie in the fact that it is Pakistan's key military ally, particularly since that country's nuclear program forced the United States to maintain its distance for most of the past decade. China is certainly in a position to put the squeeze on Pakistan's leadership, but much may depend on Beijing's attitude to any direct U.S. intervention in Afghanistan.

Tajikistan, the former Soviet republic whose 6 million people share strong ethnic ties with Afghan Tajiks, has long been engaged in Afghanistan, particularly as a key rear base of opposition activity. Wracked by internal conflict, it continues to allow a Russian military presence and has been the staging ground for Russian assistance to Afghan opposition groups. Tajikistan could be an important staging ground for any U.S. military action in Afghanistan – if Russia gives its approval, which remains an open question.

Uzbekistan, another former Soviet republic whose 25 million people share ethnic ties with an anti-Taliban section of the Afghan population, faces an Islamist insurgency of its own, and that intensifies its opposition to Afghanistan's ruling militia. It has served as a rear base for opposition forces based in the north and could be another important base for U.S. action – once again, if its Russian patron is willing.

Turkmenistan, the third former Soviet republic bordering Afghanistan, is less engaged with events across the border. It appears reluctant to get involved and, like its neighboring "stans," won't act without Moscow's say-so.

Iran is implacably hostile to the Taliban over that movement's extremist theology and over its killing of Afghan Shiite Muslims. In 1999, Iran almost went to war against the Taliban after its militia killed eight Iranian diplomats and a journalist after capturing a predominantly Shiite town and has worked together with Russia to support anti-Taliban opposition forces. Despite the overtures between the reformist President Mohammed Khatami and the West on ways of cooperating against terrorism, hard-line spiritual leader Ayatollah Khamenei insisted that while Iran condemned the terror strikes in the United States, Tehran could not support U.S. military action against Afghanistan. Still, whether working directly with the United States or not, Iran remains a key regional player in the anti-Taliban alliance.

## EXPERTS PONDER CAUSE OF COLLAPSE

*Though of lesser importance than the tragic, overwhelming human losses, the loss of the buildings was also shocking. All seven buildings of the World Trade Center complex were completely destroyed. Of nearly 300 acres (120 hectares) of commercial space, only a small portion of the north Plaza building still encloses recognizable space.*

The list of collapsed buildings includes WTC 6, the U.S. Customs House to the north; WTC 3, the twenty-two-story Marriott World Trade Center hotel just west of Tower Two; and WTC 4 and 5, the south and north Plaza buildings to the east. Insurance companies estimated their costs for the World Trade Center disaster at about $30 billion.

The north tower, called One World Trade Center, was hit at 8:45 A.M.; the south tower, Two World Trade Center, at 9:03 A.M. Another hijacked airliner, a Boeing 757 with sixty-four people on board, crashed into a section of the Pentagon at 9:40 A.M.

There is considerable speculation as to the cause of the collapses. Most engineers believe they occurred as a result of a combination of extraordinary events, including the initial aircraft impacts and implosions, which destroyed part of the structures, and the subsequent deadly fire, which gradually crippled what remained. The collapses may have transpired when the weight of the buildings above the points of collision exceeded the reduced-load carrying capacity of the remaining structure. It is speculated that the collapse of the forty-seven-story building adjacent to the Twin Towers was brought on by a deterioration of its foundations and structure from the falling towers and fire.

Reports indicate that the impact of each plane weakened the structural integrity of each tower, destroying perimeter columns and the interior structures. Further damage was sustained as the explosions swept through several floors. Experts say the fuel content of the airliners, slated for long flights, generated the massive explosions, which no building could have withstood.

"It was the fire that killed the buildings. There's nothing on Earth that could survive those temperatures with that amount of fuel burning," said structural engineer Chris Wise. "The columns would have melted, the floors would have melted, and eventually they would have collapsed one on top of each other."

When the hijacked planes, filled with fuel for cross-country flights, struck the towers, the rupture of the fuel tanks started an extremely hot fire that weakened the buildings' structural steel and caused the buildings' deadly crumpling.

No building could have survived such a blow, expert after expert have said. As the fires raged, the structural steel on the affected floors and above would have softened and warped because of the intense heat. Fireproof steel is only rated to resist 1,500 to 1,600 degrees Fahrenheit. As the structure warped and weakened at the top of each tower, the frames, along with concrete slabs, furniture, file cabinets, and other materials, became immense, centralized weights that eventually demolished the lower portions of the frames below.

A big question for implosion experts is why the Twin Towers appeared to have collapsed in such different ways. Experts say the 1,362-foot-tall south tower, which was hit at about the sixtieth floor, "failed much as one would fell a tree," as was to be expected. But the 1,368-foot-tall north tower, similarly hit but at about the ninetieth floor, "failed vertically" — the upper floor fell upon the floors below — rather than toppling over. They have no idea of the cause of the "telescoping." The design of the World Trade Center saved thousands of lives by standing for well over an hour after the planes crashed into its Twin Towers, allowing people to escape.

The building's construction manager, Hyman Brown, agreed that nothing could have saved the towers from the inferno. "This building would have stood had a plane or a force caused by a plane smashed into it, but not the fire," he said.

What immediately grabbed Brown's attention was the terrorists' seeming perception in knowing exactly where to strike. If the planes had struck too high, the weight of the melted upper floors wouldn't have been sufficient to collapse the building. And if the planes had struck too low, firefighters might not have been able to contain the fire before the steel melted. "They knew to wipe out the corner staircase, what floors to strike, and how many gallons of gas [to use to fuel the fire]. The reality is that not one part of this was an accident," he told reporters.

Many questions remain unanswered: No expert has explained why One World Trade Center remained standing for one hour and forty minutes while Two World Trade Center tumbled just fifty-six minutes after impact. Another mystery is why smaller, neighboring structures remained intact even though fire and steel from the Twin Towers rained down on them and even removed huge chunks from their facades.

## THE MAN WHO SUPERVISED THE CONSTRUCTION

*From an article by Chris Barge*
*(The Daily Camera, September 12, 2001)*
*Reprinted with permission*

*The man who supervised construction of the World Trade Center's 110-foot Twin Towers felt confusion, then anger, then sadness Tuesday morning as he watched his masterpiece crumble on a television screen in his Boulder [Colorado] home.*

Hyman Brown, fifty-nine, a University of Colorado civil engineering professor and the Trade Center's construction manager, said the towers were destroyed in the only way imaginable. He speculated that flames, fueled by thousands of gallons of aviation fuel, melted steel supports, causing the collapse.

"Prior to seven o'clock this morning, I would have told you there's no way you could bring that building down," Brown said. "What you don't plan for is twenty-four thousand gallons of jet fuel. As far as I know, it's never been thought of."

Experts in skyscraper construction said a video of the collapse led them to think the towers were perhaps weakened by the initial impact of the airplanes that hit them Tuesday, but that heat from the resulting fires were likely the most punishing blows. But to Brown's mind, fire was the sole cause of the buildings' collapse.

"It was overdesigned to withstand almost anything," including hurricanes, high winds, and bombings, the Brooklyn native said.

For seven years, starting in 1967 as a promising twenty-seven-year-old civil engineer, Brown coordinated the construction of New York's first 100-story plus buildings since the 1927 construction of the Empire State Building. The New York Port Authority had hired Brown's boss, Tishman Realty and Construction Co., to supervise all aspects of the project, from the architect to the engineer to the structural experts. Tishman put Brown in charge.

"They were building some of the biggies," Brown said of Tishman. "And that's what I wanted to do. It was exciting."

The building Brown built contained 130,000 tons of steel. The steel alone took four years to weld in place. The skeleton featured a giant steel lattice-work "tube" at its core.

As he watched his wide-screen television Tuesday morning, Brown said he assumed the first plane crashed into one of the towers by accident.

"When the second one went in, I realized this couldn't be an accident," he said. "Then anger took over and I said, "This is a terrorist attack." Then there was sadness. I realized there's got to be ten thousand deaths. Then the buildings collapsed."

His engineer's mind went to work on the numbers. An average fifty thousand people go to work in the Twin Towers every morning. Based on the timings of the explosions, he estimated 40 percent had died. Then he figured hundreds more were killed when the rubble struck as many as seventeen neighboring buildings.

He tried to phone some of the five hundred people he knows who work in the towers. All circuits into New York were busy.

"With five hundred friends in the building, for me to believe that all of them lived is absolutely naive, but I'm going to believe it until I hear otherwise," he said.

Brown said he hopes someone reconstructs the towers.

"I think if we don't rebuild it, we're saying, 'You beat us,'" he said.

Brown's estimated cost to replace both towers: $3 billion.

*Brown, who grew up in Brooklyn, living first in Williamsburg and then Flatbush, graduated from Brooklyn Technical High School and earned an engineering degree from CCNY in 1964. After the World Trade Center was completed, Tishman Realty and Construction was awarded the contract for Disneyland, and Brown relocated to California, where he assumed the position of vice president of the com-*

*pany. In 1992, Brown left Los Angeles and moved to Boulder, Colorado, with his wife, a Ph.D. student of Holocaust studies at CU.*

## IS AMERICA'S ROMANCE WITH THE SKYSCRAPER OVER?

*Excerpt from an article by Robert Campbell and Peter Vanderwarker*
*(The Boston Globe, October 14, 2001)*
*Reprinted with permission*

*"It must be a proud and soaring thing rising in sheer exultation," said Louis Sullivan of the skyscraper.*

Sullivan knew what he was talking about. One of America's great architects, he designed the first skyscrapers that looked like something better than a vertical pile of ten small buildings. His Wainwright Building in St. Louis and Guaranty Building in Buffalo, both from the 1890s, are still among the classic skyscrapers. But the skyscraper wasn't only proud and soaring. It was something else, too. It was American.

The skyscraper was invented in this country, in New York and Chicago. It became as powerful a symbol of America as the Stars and Stripes or the Statue of Liberty. That is one reason why, on September 11, terrorists chose the World Trade Center as a building they wanted to hit. Knocking off the loftiest building in New York was a way of knocking off America itself. America no longer stood tall.

Skyscrapers are part of our national myth.... A skyscraper is tall, strong, silent, lone, and self-reliant.... It is silhouetted against the sky. Skyscrapers aren't sociable buildings that collect into chatty neighborhoods, like Boston's bow-front town houses. They're a symbol, instead, of our technology, our ambition, our independence.

They're also ever present in the national psyche. We love them, but they scare us a little, too.... [People] tend to see skyscrapers as one of two things: either towers that are vulnerable to being knocked down, thus symbolizing wider destruction, or else claustrophobic interiors in which we may become trapped.

One of us happened to be in Amsterdam on the day of the attack. A Dutch friend there said, "New York will never look like New York again." The remark at first sounded strange. When we ourselves think of New York, we don't think of skylines.... But to our Dutch friend New York was an image, an emerald city of myth rather than a place he'd actually lived in. And the image was that of a skyline. The gleaming silver towers were the climax of that skyline. For him, New York has been robbed of its crown jewels.

The truth, though, is that the World Trade Center towers really weren't "proud and soaring things." Few architects liked them. Unlike such older towers as the Chrysler Building or the Empire State Building, they didn't seem to be reaching for the clouds in aspiration. They were just big boxes. They looked like the crates the real towers came in that someone forgot to unpack. They were so big that they threw the rest of Manhattan out of scale, destroying the famous skyline by trivializing it.

Before the WTC, Manhattan was like a cluster of mountain

peaks with foothills around them, one of the most exciting urban forms in the world. After the WTC, those older towers looked like mere underbrush beneath the huge and overbearing newcomer. Buildings are always, whatever else they are, billboards bearing messages. And the message of the WTC was "We're just boxes of leasable space, nothing more. We're all about commerce, about doing business."

They transformed a poetic, romantic skyline into a sort of bar graph of wealth and power. Surely this is one more reason they were singled out by terrorists. They were billboards of corporate and economic power, a power we Americans sometimes exercise insensitively.

Skyscrapers are the latest manifestation of a law of Western culture. It's this: Whoever has the most power in a society gets to build the tallest building. A famous example is the family towers of the little town of San Gimignano in Italy, where, starting about 1300, each wealthy family built an entirely useless tower for no better reason than a lust to outdo the neighbors. This tiny place once boasted seventy high-rise brick towers, some of them as tall as 175 feet, higher than Niagara Falls. In other cities, the palace of the king or duke might be the tallest building. In the Middle Ages, when the church was at its strongest, it was the cathedrals that dominated the skyline.

The story of the skyscraper is the story of San Gimignano writ large. Erecting skyscrapers became a kind of sporting event, a challenge to see who could go highest. Chicago built them first. That was partly because the Loop constrained the size of the downtown, and developers had to go high to gain floor space. But it was also because Chicago — "city of the big shoulders," in the words of poet Carl Sandburg — was flexing its muscles at New York. Later the title passed to New York, then back to Chicago. Developers competed to build the highest.

The first recognized world title holder was the Woolworth Building in New York, in 1913, at forty-eight stories and 797 feet. It's still an impressive work. Then, in the years around 1930, New York sprouted dozens of what still make up the greatest group of skyscrapers anywhere. The Chrysler Building, the usual favorite of architects and historians, held the title of tallest in the world for a few months in 1930–31. But it was quickly surpassed by the Empire State Building, 102 stories and 1,250 feet, which held the world championship for a record forty-one years. "How high can you make it so it won't fall down?" was the question Empire State Building owner Jacob Raskob asked his architects, Shreve, Lamb & Harmon.

Sometimes we forget the energy of our forebears. They built the Empire State from scratch in fourteen months, its steel frame held together by rivets that were heated over little fires — remember, this is by people working in an open steel frame maybe 1,000 feet in the air — until they were red hot, then hammered into place. They built strong, too. In 1945, a B-25 bomber accidentally crashed into the seventy-ninth floor, killing fourteen but leaving the structure undamaged. When the World Trade Center took its first hit, most people assumed the same thing had happened.

After that early-'30s spurt came the Great Depression and then World War II. For a time, no one was building much. It wasn't until around 1970 that we saw another round in the competitive sport of skyscraper-building. The World Trade Center arrived in 1972, 110 stories and 1,368 feet. It held the title until Chicago grabbed it with the Sears Tower of 1974, at 1,450 feet. During the same era came the 100-story Hancock Center in Chicago, as well as Boston's Prudential and our own local champion, the all-glass, 790-foot Hancock Tower of 1976, a building that is world-renowned for its icy beauty (Henry Cobb, partner of I. M. Pei, was the architect).

All of these represented a different kind of architecture from the earlier skyscrapers. The early ones were imitations of mountains, craggy objects that got thinner at the top and seemed, like rockets, to be reaching heavenward. Partly that shape was a response to zoning laws. To let daylight into the streets, New York and other cities passed rules that required high buildings to step back as they rose. The towers of the 1960s and '70s, by contrast, were boxes with flat walls and roofs, often with minimal detail. Their method of letting sunlight down was to create an open plaza next to the tower.

The icon was the Seagram Building of 1958, by a famous modernist architect, Mies van der Rohe (even today, there are two major shows of Mies' work on display in New York, at the Whitney and the Museum of Modern Art). The Seagram is the prototype of the postwar skyscraper, a simple (although subtle) box in shape, with an invisible steel frame inside to hold it up and a skin of tinted glass, delicately gridded, that is hung from the frame and therefore known as a "curtain wall."

The Seagram is a handsome object, but when its ilk began to multiply in city after city, American architecture suddenly seemed monotonous, abstract, and lacking in craft. In the 1970s, architects began to look for ways to jazz up these monotonous boxes. This explains the odd Gothic-style arches at the base of the World Trade Center, frilly motifs that looked like doilies against the vast bulk of the towers.

After the Sears Tower, America went on building skyscrapers. But we stopped being contenders. The action shifted elsewhere. Of the world's twenty tallest skyscrapers today, not a single one was built in the United States in the final twenty-five years of the twentieth century. Among Americans, only The Donald continues to trumpet the virtues of building a world's tallest. The title is now held by the twin-peaked Petronas Towers in Kuala Lumpur, Malaysia, designed by American architect Cesar Pelli, at only eighty-eight stories but 1,483 feet. Of today's top twenty, ten are in Southeast Asia, and three more are in the Middle East. Europe's tallest, the Commerzbank in Frankfurt, by Briton Norman Foster (the architect of proposed additions to the Museum of Fine Arts in Boston), ranks only twenty-ninth internationally.

Why are Asians and Middle Easterners building skyscrapers? Are they deliberately going glove to glove with America, the way Chicago once took on New York? Or is it that the skyscraper is now a cultural symbol of something larger? A symbol, perhaps, that a nation, a city, or a corporation has arrived to take its place on the global politico-economic game board?

Americans are inventors, and the skyscraper appeared here first largely because Americans invented three things that made it possible: the steel frame, the elevator, and the electric light. Before the steel frame, you made a tall building by piling stones one upon the other. The walls held up the building and were called bearing walls. The Ames Building (1889) on Court Street in Boston, one of the last of the breed, has walls nine feet thick at the base. At thirteen stories, it remains the second tallest bearing-wall building in the world.

Only four years later and two blocks away, a new technology arrived. The Winthrop Building at 7 Water Street was the first Boston building to be held up by an interior skeleton of steel. It is revolutionary and beautiful. The Winthrop is thin, it curves to match the street, and its ground floor features delicate steel columns framing huge windows. With a steel frame, you could clip on glass windows and metal panels to make the skin of the building. Result: the shimmering tower. It is only a step, technically speaking, from the Winthrop Building to the Hancock Tower, with its ultimate minimal surface of 10,344 identical glass rectangles.

Steel skeletons alone wouldn't have made skyscrapers possible. But in 1857 the first passenger elevator was installed in a New York building known as the Haughwout Store. "At a stroke," writes historian Carter Wiseman, "the tall building was flung open to those who were not alpinists." Because of the elevator, the top floors of a building became the most valuable, thanks to their fine views. The higher you went, the better the view, or so it was thought. Elevators make height possible, but past a certain point they take up so much of the rentable floor space that buildings become less efficient. At the WTC, there were 104 passenger elevators in each tower. Another invention, the electric light (Thomas Edison, 1879), made it possible to illuminate the new, large interior spaces.

The steel frame has its limits, too. Above about eighty stories, the wind loads on skyscrapers exert more stress on the steel frame than does the weight of the building. Architects and engineers experimented with new technologies. Fazlur Kahn, a structural engineer in Chicago, invented a structure he called "bundled tubes" and employed it on the Sears Tower.

The World Trade Center, too, was a tube structure. It was designed by Minoru Yamasaki, an architect prominent enough to have his picture on the cover of *Time* magazine in 1963. Instead of being clothed in a curtain wall of glass hung off an interior skeleton, the WTC was held up by its exterior wall, much like the bearing-wall buildings of the past. The wall, which wrapped the towers, was a sort of fence of closely spaced steel columns, with windows between them. Together with the internal elevator core, this skin is what held the building up. Experts say there is no reason to think the innovative structure was any more vulnerable to attack than a conventional frame would have been.

Yamasaki was admired in his day for bringing a kind of pictorial prettiness to modern architecture. He designed two buildings at Harvard, William James Hall on Kirkland Street and the Engineering Sciences Laboratory on Oxford, as well as the more noteworthy Woodrow Wilson School at Princeton. All three are white, temple-like structures that seem to ignore everything around them. Historian Bainbridge Bunting got it right in his book *Harvard: An Architectural History* when he wrote, "High-rise buildings do not have to stand out like sore thumbs...but William James Hall does so." He could just as well have been talking about the WTC. Another Yamasaki building was the Pruitt-Igoe low-income housing project of 1955, in St. Louis. The Pruitt-Igoe towers proved to be such a failure that, in an eerie precursor to the fate of the WTC, they were intentionally dynamited by the city in 1972, the very year the WTC opened.

In the haunting photographs taken after the collapse of the World Trade towers, the only things still standing are pieces of the exterior steel structure. They look like fallen sections of a picket fence, but once they supported two great towers. Perhaps the best memorial to the disaster would be to bring one of them back, repositioned just as it was, tilted and fallen.

In the aftermath of the WTC disaster, will we stop building skyscrapers? Will people be afraid to work in them? Were skyscrapers ever particularly good places to work? For some, perhaps they were. We all know the image: the captain of industry, standing in his penthouse office, silhouetted in thought against the perfect view of New York. He's at the pinnacle of power, far above the chaos and dirt of the street.

We asked a friend of ours what it is like to work up high. She has worked in the Hancock Tower for twenty-five years, most of the time on the fifty-eighth floor. Recently she moved to floor 22, where she looks out over Copley Square. She's much happier there, she says, because she feels she is part of the city in which she works. On floor 58, when she looked out of the window, there was no foreground. There was a purely distant view. The window might as well have been a painted mural. And not everyone, of course, even gets a window.

That's one thing that is sure to change. In most of Europe,

it is now the law that every worker must be within about seven meters (roughly twenty feet) of a window. European skyscrapers are "greener" than ours, too. They explore ways to save energy and other resources. They are typically slim and transparent, and their glass walls are often enlivened with visually interesting sun-control systems. They are the opposite of the huge flat boxes of the WTC, in which every floor was nearly one acre in area (about the size of a football field) and where workers were often far from daylight. As we face up to the crisis of global warming and other demands on planetary resources, America will surely move in the same direction as Europe. There is no way that the WTC could be built, or should be built, in our own time.

With skyscrapers, too, the surrounding city pays a price. The windswept plazas of Chicago, New York, and Boston can be dark, freezing, and even dangerous in high winds. The streets around tall buildings are often dead, because the employees are commuters from the suburbs who drive into an underground garage and ride an elevator to their offices. Overbearing towers can be alienating and can make a pedestrian feel intimidated. The sleek glass-and-metal curtain walls feel like the wrappings of a consumer culture. Working in such a tower, you can feel cut off from the world. The best towers are those that reach out to greet the public on the sidewalk with shops and restaurants. The older skyscrapers — the Chrysler, the Empire State — did that, so much so that you're hardly aware of the tower except as seen from a distance. The real life of great cities, always, is the life of the street.

Symbolism aside, skyscrapers have one real virtue. They

create high density: a lot of building in a small area. Density makes it possible for an enormous number of people to work in walkable proximity to one another, as in midtown Manhattan, and that's good for business, for urban excitement, and for the creative exchange of ideas. Some now argue that the cyberworld makes that kind of proximity unnecessary, but we don't agree. High density is fuel-efficient, too, compared with the sprawl of suburban office parks.

But as many studies have shown, high densities can be achieved without skyscrapers. Paris is the most densely built city in the Western world by far, yet it has few towers and many parks and boulevards. We're guessing that high-density, mixed-use, mid-rise buildings, more on the Paris model, will be the wave of the immediate future.

Cities, in any case, are changing. More than ever, they are now places of leisure and culture rather than business and industry. The defining building of the last ten years is the art museum in Bilbao, Spain, by American architect Frank Gehry, where tourists flock simply to experience the architecture. Perhaps the next crop of image makers for our cities will be the cultural leaders, not the business leaders. The skyline of commercial towers may be supplanted as the image of the city, replaced by the icons of culture and entertainment. Gehry is designing another amazing museum for the Guggenheim, this one in New York. It will blossom out over the East River in Manhattan like a four-block-wide titanium flower.

As thrill makers, in short, skyscrapers may be obsolete. Our parents took us to the top of the Empire State Building as a rite of passage. There will always be excitement associated with height, but now it may occur elsewhere than in office buildings. The observation deck of the John Hancock closed permanently right after September 11. In London, the way to get high is the London Eye, a five-hundred-foot Ferris wheel on the banks of the Thames. The huge wheel turns continuously, very slowly. You step on and watch as the city and the Thames shrink beneath you. It's a thrill, especially at dusk. Who needs office-tower observation decks?

The debate is under way about what to build at the site of the World Trade Center. The skyscraper is one of the great . American inventions. We may be done with skyscraping, but we will never stop inventing.

# SPEECH FROM NEW YORK STATE GOVERNOR GEORGE E. PATAKI TO THE JOINT SESSION OF THE STATE LEGISLATURE

*Today we join together as a state, and as a nation, to pray for the victims who were lost on one of the darkest days in American history.*

We pray for the children who will go to bed this evening without their mothers and fathers. We pray for the mothers and fathers who've lost the children they loved.

We pray for the husbands and wives who will return to empty homes. We pray for the firefighters, police officers, and rescue workers who died while committing extraordinary acts of heroism. We pray, also, for this great nation of ours, a nation that is free, a nation that is strong, a nation that is united in grief. For we know that the freedom we so cherish for which countless thousands have sacrificed their lives exposes us to the wicked, the murderous, the cowardly forces of hate.

December 7th will always be known as a "day of infamy." So, too, September 11th, forever will be known as the day a dark cloud descended across America.

But clouds always pass. The sun always breaks through. And we know as Americans that God's light will again shine across this great land and that our free and strong people will prevail.

The forces of evil that committed this atrocity have caused pain that will last for generations, pain that has claimed the lives of innocent men, women, and children. But evil never prevails. Freedom, despite its vulnerabilities, will always prevail.

And I am confident that President Bush and a united American Congress will strike back — swiftly and strongly — against the forces of terror and the nations that harbor them. We will stand with the president in those actions.

New Yorkers have always stood strong, firm, and together in times of crisis and human hardship. Already we've seen the extraordinary heroism of our firefighters, police officers, emergency service workers, and everyday citizens. We've seen the indomitable spirit of New Yorkers, pulling together to overcome the most horrendous, destructive, and murderous act of terrorism in history. We owe a deep debt of gratitude for the heroism of the thousands who have been risking, and continue to risk, their lives to help with the relief effort.

We thank President Bush for the extraordinary aid he has provided. And we owe profound thanks to Mayor Giuliani, and to his team, for the tremendous leadership they have shown.

This crisis has tested and will continue to test the resolve and the resilience of New Yorkers like never before. But ultimately the courageous and resilient spirit of our people will prevail over this cowardly act of hatred.

Yesterday I was at Bellevue Hospital visiting injured firefighters. I stood at the bedside of a lieutenant, thanked him for his courage, and told him he was a hero. He smiled and said, in a thick New York accent, "What'd you expect? I'm a New Yorker."

But then the smile left his face as he spoke about his partner, who was missing. With tears in his eyes, he told me his partner was the father of ten children.

I told him that those children will not be alone. We will stand with them. We will stand with all of these heroes, and we will stand with the children and family members they left behind.

They are now a part of us. They will be a part of New York, and America, forever.

The people of this state are united as never before. I've seen New Yorkers lined up for blocks, waiting to donate blood at Cabrini Hospital. I asked one woman why she was there, and she said, "I have to be here." I've seen injured firefighters at St. Vincent's, begging to leave their hospital beds, so they could go back and rejoin their comrades in the rescue effort. All across our state people are volunteering to help however and wherever they can. In this time of crisis, we can draw strength from that spirit of unity and from the compassion of our people.

There is nothing we cannot accomplish when we are united behind a common purpose. It is that common purpose that brings us here today. For today the issues that occasionally divide seem small.

Today we are united in our commitment to rebuild the greatest city in the world. And we are united in our commitment to rekindle the spirit of our people. And because we are unified, I know we will be unanimous in the action we take today to begin putting this crisis behind us.

Make no mistake: We will not just survive this disaster. Nor will we simply overcome it. We, the people of New York, will join together, united in strength, and lift New York to its greatest day. We face a long and difficult road. But we face it together.

These unspeakable acts have shattered our city and shocked our nation. But they have not weakened the bonds that unite us as New Yorkers, as Americans, as those who love freedom, and, ultimately, as those who love one another.

Our strength will defeat this evil. Our spirit will overcome this atrocity. And together, this land of the people, and by the people, will soar higher than even our beloved Twin Towers.

## WHERE WAS GOD?

*By S. Barole*

*I've been hearing people ask, "Where was God when the World Trade Center and the Pentagon were attacked?" I'm sure I know.*

H e was finding ways to prevent people from boarding those airplanes. Those four flights had the capacity to hold 1,000 passengers, but only 266 were aboard. He was calming the frightened passengers on the four flights. No family member receiving a call from a loved one recalled hearing a cracked voice. On one of the flights He was giving the passengers courage to try to subdue the hijackers.

He was creating reasons for employees at the World Trade Center to be late for work or absent. Only around twenty thousand were at the towers when the first jet hit. Since over fifty thousand worked there, in addition to tens of thousands of visitors, this was a miracle in itself.

He was holding up the two 110-story buildings until two-thirds of the workers escaped. Wasn't it incredible that the top of the towers didn't fall when the jets crashed into the buildings? And when they finally fell, they fell inward. He didn't allow the towers to topple over, because many more people would have been killed.

And when the buildings collapsed, He took the souls of the victims and brought them to their place of rest, showing them that the worst was over and their reward was in store.

He sent the people who were experienced and trained for disaster relief and mobilized them to save the few who were were still alive, even though they themselves would not survive. And He dispatched thousands of others to volunteer their help in other ways.

He was getting burn victims to New York Presbyterian Hospital, home of the nation's leading burn unit, which by perverse "happenstance" was located only about a hundred blocks from Ground Zero.

He was helping survivors find places to take shelter until they were physically and mentally able to wend their way home, and He found ways for them to get there.

And He still isn't finished. He comforts the loved ones, young and old, who were left bereaved. His sends his messengers to come to their aid and to give them moral support. And He will take care of us whatever the future may bring.

He will bestow upon the leaders of this country the courage and the judgment to do the right thing. Although He has sent us a wake-up call, He will never desert us.

Although this is the worst calamity this country has ever witnessed, God's miracles pervade every second of it. It is difficult to imagine what it would be like to live through this tragedy without believing in God. Life would be unbearable.

# A DANGEROUS PLACE

*From an editorial (Jewish Forward, September 14, 2001)*
*Reprinted with permission*

*Faced with the horrifying realities of September 11 – our cities covered in ashes, our national symbols reduced to rubble, our fellow citizens slaughtered – Americans found themselves groping for words this week, struggling to give voice to something we had never before experienced. One thing, though, was instantly clear: our security had been breached.*

No, not just the defenses meant to guard our borders. The terrorists who hijacked four airliners packed with innocents and turned them into flying bombs breached America's sense of herself. They stripped away her magnificent isolation, dried up the oceans that protected her, brought her with a brutal thud into the global village with all its squalor and danger.

It is a dangerous place, this global village. We knew that before, but we did not understand it. Americans have spoken the words "dangerous place" with regularity over the years, yet we spoke too lightly. Often we spoke with a dismissive sneer, as though the world were some other place across the sea. The words will no longer come so lightly. From now on, when we speak about the world, we are speaking of ourselves.

President Bush was right to describe the attacks as an "act of war" and to pledge an American fight to victory in what he called a "monumental struggle of good versus evil." The unspeakable savagery of the terrorists, the diabolical scope of their deeds, the terrible losses in America's main cities, permit no other description. The perpetrators of these inhuman acts must be found and brought down.

The challenge before us is to maintain our own humanity in the midst of this battle. Up to now America has fought terror using the dainty tools of law enforcement — arrest warrants, extradition hearings, jury trials. That route has failed. This is war. But it is a war unlike any we have fought before. It is a shadow war fought against a shadowy enemy who makes no distinction between civilian and military targets and defies the civilized world to maintain that distinction.

A war against terror means a constant struggle to avoid being reduced to the moral depravity of the terrorists themselves — for that way lies chaos, which is the terrorists' goal. That is the dilemma with which Israel has grappled for years, alone and largely misunderstood. Perhaps America's horror will help bring home to the West the depth of the dilemma Israel has faced over the years.

Whatever the challenge to Americans, the terror poses a special challenge to American Jews. For the deadly assault on New York City was not meant merely as a symbolic blow against America's media and finance center. As they have made clear repeatedly over the last decade, in intercepted messages and in testimony in open court, Islamic extremists view New York as the capital of world Jewry and a good place to kill Jews. Their previous efforts were largely ineffectual. This week they succeeded spectacularly.

Most of us find this truth painful, even dangerous. Painful because it reminds us of our vulnerability here in the land where Jews have found such safety. Dangerous because we fear our fellow Americans will blame us for the troubles that face us all, as if abandoning the Jews might make non-Jews safer.

But America is better than that. As New Yorkers declared repeatedly on the streets this week, they understand that the terrorists' war against America is at least partly due to America's alliance with Israel, and it does not faze them. They showed, as Americans have shown repeatedly over the years, that they are ready to stand with their friends and against their enemies. Americans will not be divided.

The extent of the losses in the destruction of the World Trade Center will not be known in full for days, perhaps weeks, but it seemed clear this week that the final tally would be in the thousands. The crime dwarfs any single act of peacetime violence in memory. As the full extent of the calamity becomes clearer, the steely resolve shown around New York and across America in the first days after the disaster will give way to deeper levels of grief and anger. As emotions surge, we must hold fast to our humanity and our faith in our fellow Americans. The real test is yet to come.

# AMERICA DECEIVED AGAIN

*By Vincent J. Tómeo (January 19, 2002)*

To me 9.11.01 is the worst event in American history.
To see my nation sneak-attacked...
To see the Towers burning from my window
To smell death from my house
To see my world in smoke
To see freedom slapped in the face
Stabbed in the back
Stepped on
Knocked down...
To think I knew an al Qaeda cell
Who owned a Dunkin' Donuts coffee shop
On Roosevelt Avenue
Between Main and Prince Streets in Flushing, Queens
To know
I looked into the eyes of someone
Who would plot my death hurts me
The FBI said
This Dunkin' Donuts owner closed his shop
And left the U.S. several days before September 11, 2001

Today this Dunkin' Donuts is still closed
To think I looked into the eyes of evil and did not know the
   difference.

# A 911 ACROSTIC

*by Rabbi Yosef Chaim Schwab*
*Maggid shiur, kiruv professional,*
*and director of Torah Shiurim, World Torah Radio*

T   he hit was direct; it left its impression.
H   olocaust of death, Gehinnom in session.
E   verywhere resounded a rude wake-up call

T   o return to values, to stand up tall.
W   ith the Creator's message, to a nation now oppressed,
I   n Ninveh fashion, to elevate man to his best.
N   o time in history was a land so humane

T   orah and mitzvos are granted free rein.
O   utsiders saw U.S. as evil and decadent
W   hen in truth acts of *chessed* are widely prevalent.
E   ach true American is proof of *nishmas chaim*
R   esembling *chassidei umos ha'olam*, really trying.
S   o our *puraniyos* inspired faith in Almighty God

N   ot just a day of prayer, but acceptance of His rod.
I   n this terrible act of terror were signs of benevolence
N   o tower or plane full, thanks to His Providence.
E   very madman has his day, his moment of glee.

E  ach act of *hashgachah*, too awesome to see.
L  ost souls are returning with vigor and force,
E  xamining their lifestyle, returning to the Source.
V  ery soon we will hear *besuros tovos*, I'm sure
E  ach heart will rejoice and be sad no more.
N  ow is the time for *teshuvah* as never before.

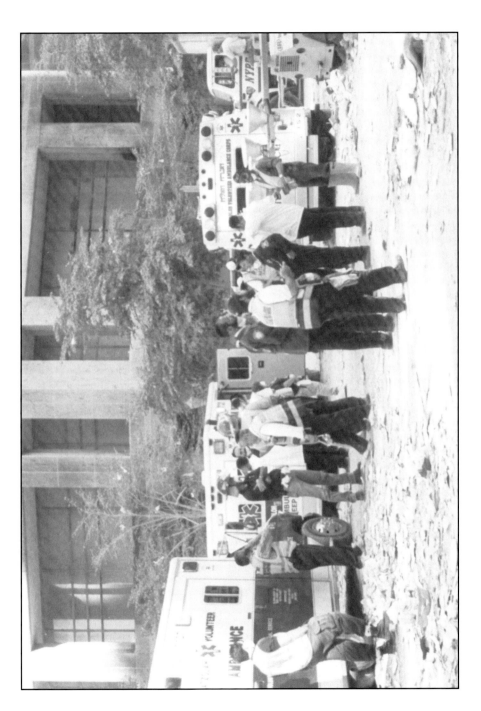

# The Horror

## CITY OF GHOSTS

By Tom Robins and Jennifer Gonnerman, with additional reporting
by Toni Schlesinger, Emma Nwegbo, James Wong, and Carla Spartos
(Village Voice, week of September 19–25, 2001)
Reprinted with permission

*At 9:59 on the morning of Day One, with the collapse of the
first World Trade Center tower, a rain of fine gray dust began settling on lower Manhattan. It coated the streets and
cars, the trapped rescue vehicles, the trees in the parks, the
late summer flowers, the faces and clothes of the panicky
citizens rushing for their lives; it nestled on the hats and
helmets of the police and firefighters and into the hair of
the emergency medical workers.*

The rain thickened thirty minutes later with the fall of the
second tower, leaving a dusty carpet inches thick on the
gleaming new glass financial houses in Battery Park
City, on the restored fountain in front of City Hall, on the old,
narrow, crooked streets of the financial district, the ones that
drove Melville's Bartleby mad with their looming high walls.

The ash could be seen rising from the angry red and yellow flames that raged high above the city after the demon airplanes struck. It was carried on billowing clouds of black smoke that rose into a bright blue sky where a faint half-moon still hung, the last emblem of the innocent night before. A steady northwest breeze steered it over the harbor, past Governor's Island into Brooklyn and the Atlantic Ocean beyond.

In the hours after the terrible cataclysm, those trodding through the lower Manhattan streets, their footsteps muffled as though in fresh snow, realized the powder that some called ash and soot was also made of something else: concrete dust. It was the buildings themselves, pulverized by the billions of pounds of downward pressure generated by the collapse.

What had that impossible event felt like close up? "First, this tremendous wind. Then it was like you put your hand inside a sand castle. It just crumbled," said Felix Sanchez, forty-six, who, with two dozen coworkers, ran thirty blocks to the site to help.

Some 425,000 cubic yards of concrete were poured into the Twin Towers as they rose in the late 1960s. Concrete formed the thick slabs dividing the 110 floors of each building and was also poured seventy feet deep into the ground to hold the mighty steel beams that supported the buildings' vertical loads. It was enough concrete, as its builders then proudly proclaimed, to pave a five-foot-wide sidewalk all the way from Manhattan to Washington, D.C.

"The scale was cyclopean," said Eric Darton, who wrote a critical history of the towers two years ago and watched their final chapter from the windows of his doctor's office on Tuesday.

More than 1.2 million cubic yards of earth and rock were excavated to make way for the World Trade Center. More than 200,000 tons of steel were used, each beam weighing fifty-two tons. There were 43,600 narrow windows — containing 600,000 square feet of glass. When the building was completed, every inch of pane was cleaned by automatic machines that moved vertically along stainless steel tracks. There were ninety-nine elevators, arranged by zones so that no trip took more than two minutes. Five million square feet of painted gypsum board formed interiors, along with 7 million square feet of acoustical tiles, 200,000 lighting fixtures, 40,000 doorknobs, 1,200 soap dispensers.

It was so rock solid then: a pair of 1,350-foot-tall monuments visible on clear days from Bear Mountain in the north to Sandy Hook in the south. They were a guide and compass for anyone lost in the city. They were the gargantuan presence against which all large things were measured. "As big as the World Trade Center" was a universal yardstick. When King Kong was remade in 1976, the gorilla's final fatal climb was shifted from the Empire State Building to the new towers. The moviemakers constructed an immense replica of the fallen beast in the plaza, surrounded by fake rubble. Office workers staring from the eightieth floor remarked how tiny the mighty Kong looked.

The Twin Towers were the first buildings to catch the rising sun, reflecting a brilliant light off their metallic finish. Israeli-born architect Eli Attia, who designed the sleek Millennium Hilton Hotel across Church Street from the Trade Center, was awakened every morning in his Brooklyn bedroom by the light. "Winter or summer, the reflected light from the towers filled our windows," he said. "Toward sunset, before the electric lights came on, from a certain angle the towers resembled a pair of mammoth trees."

Great tragedies leave behind legions of ghosts. They are the ghosts of those who perished, who would otherwise walk the streets, ride the subways and buses, dine in restaurants, toil at their jobs...hold their children.... There one minute, they are suddenly disappeared, leaving only echoes, photographs, and intangible, ever-fading memories.

Insulated from the direst natural storms, modern New York City nevertheless has had its own experience with enormous loss.

None match the vast new army of ghosts created within one hundred lethal minutes between the moment the first plane struck to the collapse of the second tower on the otherwise resplendent morning of September 11.

How many died? The numbers, made purposefully vague by authorities fearful for public morale, are a moving target. On Monday, the estimate of those missing or dead stood at 5,623. Gathered together, the victims would overflow the bleachers in Yankee Stadium.

But if the horrifying numbers are still imprecise, the ghosts have already assembled. They are there in the hundreds of posters created by distraught family members and friends, taped to trees, telephone booths, mailboxes, bus shelters, and vans. More than one thousand have been attached to the plywood "Wall of Prayer" at the entrance to Bellevue Hospital, just south of the grim East Thirtieth Street offices of the city's medical examiner, where refrigerated trucks hold corpses and body parts. An astonishing number of the posters are computer-generated snapshots: pictures from weddings, from vacation cruises, from barbecues. Some are of business-men and women posing proudly in front of the tall buildings that have become their likely tomb. Some, of parents with their children, read, "Hurry home, Daddy."

The names are a New York symphony: Foti, Costello, Puckett, Barbella, Luparello, Morris, Faragher, Zinzi, Smith, Kumar, Ramos, Supinski, Bergstein, Barnes, Cho, Callahan, DeSantis, Wong, Dedvukaj, Villanueva, Cahill, Traina, Zeng. Even Rockefeller.

Likewise, the colors of the faces range from pale to dark, with every shade in between. Did the attackers imagine their victims? Did they picture the heathens they sought to punish as one class, one race, one color? If so, they failed miserably. The roster of the dead and the missing is inexorably demo-cratic. There are investment bankers, secretaries, electricians, janitors, cops, firemen, photographers, delivery workers, bond brokers, cooks, waiters, dishwashers, lawyers, painters, and accountants.

The hijackers, who were in their twenties and thirties, ap-parently did have one thing in common with many of their vic-tims: youth. "I had a very young staff," said Howard Lutnick, chairman of Cantor Fitzgerald, a bond trading company, as he tearfully described losing more than six hundred of his em-ployees.

Turn back the clock, omit those dreadful minutes, and what would everyone be doing? What would be happening in these towers and streets minus the deadly debris, crushing rubble, and the bleak gray carpet?

We know that Eliezer Jimenez, thirty-eight, would be cooking at Windows on the World, the famous restaurant where tables were arranged to afford a glorious view for all diners. That bond broker Jason Defazio, twenty-nine, might be opening the pictures from his wedding three months ago after getting a seat on the express bus from Staten Island to his job at Cantor Fitzgerald on the 104th floor of Tower One. That Elizabeth Holmes, forty-two, of Harlem, her long braids swinging, would be coming up from the IRT and starting her day with a cup of tea at her desk....

We know that Borders Books & Music at 5 World Trade Center, overlooking Vesey Street, would be preparing to host that week's guest author, browsers moving through its aisles.... We know that the concourse below the towers — the city's largest indoor mall — would be filled with people, many of them from among the fifty thousand daily commuters exiting the subways or rising on a massive bank of escalators from the New Jersey PATH trains. We know that the city's shrewdest clothing shoppers would be eagerly pawing through the racks of Century 21 across Church Street in the old bank building, where Polo shirts or, on occasion, a Galliano gown, were savagely reduced from their original prices.

We know that people would still be talking about the series of outdoor summer concerts on the plaza, where musicians...provided free entertainment under the stars. Visitors would still flock to the windswept five-acre plaza, named after Port Authority leader and Trade Center pioneer Austin J.

Tobin. Believe it or not, designers had St. Mark's Square in Venice in mind when they laid it out, encircling it with a huge Gothic arcade.

How could it all disappear so quickly? In the wake of the 1993 bombing, after the terrorists' plainspoken ringleader, Ramzi Yousef, told federal agents his goal had been to destroy the buildings, experts said this proved that the Trade Center itself, by reason of design, was virtually impregnable from that type of assault.

It was different from other buildings. For almost one hundred years, conventional skyscrapers were built with interior columns supporting the building's weight, while the outer walls were merely window dressing. The Trade Center's builders rejected that approach, using the exterior walls themselves as the load-bearing structure. "The World Trade Center buildings represent a new era," wrote officials of Tishman Construction, who managed the project. "They are the buildings of the oncoming twenty-first century."

Aside from earthquakes or floods, it's unlikely that any modern urban calamity has been personally witnessed by as many people. Businessmen in midtown high-rises and schoolchildren in Brooklyn all stared with disbelieving eyes at the first, appalling, gaping hole in the south tower, then at the mad, low descent of flight 175 across the Hudson into the second building, and finally, as both landmarks vanished before their eyes. It was a view that spurred many to valor.

Felix Sanchez, a member of District Council 9 of the Painters Union and an ex-Marine who served in Beirut, saw it clearly from the building at 85 West Fifteenth Street, where he was painting a patio. By the time he and his coworkers arrived, the second plane had struck.... A frantic cop yelled, "Give us a hand!" and Sanchez and his companions charged inside, where they began helping an emergency crew from Saint Vincents Hospital. A few minutes later he heard someone yell that the structure was falling. Then smoke and dust blackened everything.

"I couldn't see anything. None of us could," Sanchez said later as he looked at the wreckage. "I just know most of the others were no longer behind me when I got out."

In Boro Park, Brooklyn, a volunteer emergency medical worker named Bernard Gipps jumped into a Hatzalah ambulance as soon as the news of the first attack spread. Its siren screaming, the ambulance raced up the Prospect Expressway and through the Brooklyn Battery Tunnel, which deposited the crew directly under the raging fires.

"We got there and we saw two gaping holes. There were people jumping and bodies everywhere," said Gipps. His crew watched in horror as a body falling from the tower's upper floors slammed into a helmet-wearing firefighter, killing both instantly. Another fireman was killed by falling debris before he even had a chance to get out of his truck. When the first tower fell, the volunteers ran for their lives, heading west across Battery Park City to the river. Several escaped by jumping onto ferries that took them to Hoboken.

Steve Sullivan, fifty-six, was eight years retired already from the New York City Fire Department when the news reached him at home in Staten Island. He tried to drive across the Verrazano Narrows Bridge, heading for Greenwich Village to team up with his old crew, Engine Company 24 and Ladder 5, where he had worked for thirteen years. Unable to get across the bridge, he drove to a Staten Island firehouse whose members commandeered a city bus down to the St. George terminal, where they hopped the last ferry to lower Manhattan.

"We got as far as the Statue of Liberty, and we saw the second tower collapse," said Sullivan. "We had the radio on, and we heard the calls. They were trapped in their rigs. They couldn't get the doors of their trucks open. And you hear it on the radio, and there is nothing to do. They are screaming, 'I can't breathe. Help me. I can't breathe.' And you can't do anything."

Once the ferry docked, Sullivan and the other firefighters rushed to the scene, but the worst had already happened. "We found Chief Feehan, a super guy, as good as they get," said Sullivan two days later, his voice cracking as he sat, still wearing his gear, on a low brick wall in the sun outside the station house on Sixth Avenue and King Street. "We found Chief Ganci. We took them out gently. You'd find an arm in a glove with a fireman's cuff on it. A backpack. You put the arm and the backpack on the side and keep looking." The wind would blow, covering the bodies with dust, making them less recognizable. "They were like Jell-O people, no hair. It makes it a little easier somehow."

"That's John," he said, showing a visitor a picture on the bulletin board upstairs in the firehouse of a tall man with a drooping handlebar moustache and a wide grin. "He's waiting for us to find him down there."

In 1994, a terrible fire killed three members of the crew at
Ladder 5, including its captain, John Drennan. Those appalling casualties drew donations and sympathy from all over the
city. As of last week, the firehouse was missing at least eight
members in the Trade Center collapse. Their fire truck was destroyed as well, the one with the huge gold number 5, the same
one that inspired painter Charles Demuth and poet William
Carlos Williams to write about its "wheels rumbling through
the dark city." The firefighters plucked the big gold numeral
off the destroyed ladder truck and placed it on the hood of a
battered gray pickup missing its windshield. "We use that
now," said Sullivan.

On Wednesday, the day after the collapse, a young couple
from North Carolina named Tori and Mark are trying to make
their way back to the apartment they had fled on South End
Avenue in Battery Park City. On West Street, near Stuyvesant
High School, they talk their way past a cop wearing a Suffolk
County shoulder patch, then a National Guardsman. Their
shoes send up clouds of gray dust as they walk through the
park along the river. Everywhere there is the litter of millions
of pieces of paper, the burst files of a thousand destroyed offices: graphs with numbers, charts covered in Chinese letter-
ing, pink buy and sell forms from brokerage houses, stern-
sounding official letters from federal agencies.

Tori and Mark moved to the city in December from Ra-
leigh. "We just wanted to be in New York," said Tori. Mark
found a job with an investment firm. Tori planned on attending New York University. They had been concerned about
finding an apartment, but the first real estate broker they vis-

ited steered them to the high-rise building at 200 Gateway Plaza. Directly out the window, to their delight, was one of the treasures they'd sought in their move north: the Twin Towers. "We love it," said Mark, like most people in the city, still using the present tense about the monolith. "The World Trade Center is such a magnificent building, just to think that people could design and achieve something like that. It's inspiring."

There is little doubt the city will commence the job of rebuilding, filling in the view again across from their apartment. This time, like Nehemiah, the...king who rebuilt the destroyed walls of Jerusalem, workers will hold "a trowel in one hand and a sword in the other."

## BEFORE COLLAPSE, BODIES FELL LIKE RAG DOLLS FROM TOWERS

*By Donna De La Cruz, The Associated Press*
*(The Daily Camera, September 12, 2001)*
*Reprinted with permission*

*NEW YORK – As the twin giants of the skyline crumbled from their 110-story grandeur to five stories of rubble, survivors coughing up dust and eyes glazed with terror fled across bridges or simply ran through streets piling up with debris.*

The lucky ones got out alive but will carry scars on their memories forever. Clemant Lewin, a banker, said he looked from his window across the street from the towers and saw people jumping from the eightieth floor....

"I'm traumatized for life," Lewin said. "Someone needs to

take responsibility for this. This was somebody's father, this was somebody's sister, somebody's mother. We should have seen this coming. I'm disgusted."

Soon after the first terrorist-controlled jetliner sliced into one of the towers, an elevator door opened inside and there stood a man on fire.

Kenny Johannemann, a janitor, said he and another grabbed the burning man, put out the fire, and dragged him outdoors. Johannemann said he then heard the second explosion and looked up. He, too, saw people jumping from windows high up in the buildings.

"It was horrendous. I can't describe it," Johannemann said.

The two buildings stood proudly erect, but not for long.

Well before the fifty thousand people who report for work in the buildings daily would have taken lunch breaks, the landmarks telescoped down upon themselves into chunks of blackened concrete and jagged steel girders jutting only fifty feet above the street.

For blocks around, the streets became rivers of water, oil, and soot. A heavy blanket of ash, seen from miles away, hovered over lower Manhattan and showered down miles away to the east in the borough of Brooklyn.

Crumpled police cars and fire trucks with their roofs smashed, their windows blown out, dotted a trail away from the horror.

Thomas Warren, a paralegal, said he found a man dazed and stumbling out of the area wearing shoes that did not match. He had lost his in the blast and grabbed any that were handy.

As workers cleared some of the rubble, new crews of firefighters and rescue workers charged into the devastation with shovels, pickaxes, and flashlights to look for bodies or survivors.

A union official said he feared three hundred firefighters who first reached the scene had died in rescue efforts and dozens of police officers were missing.

Survivors among the first group of firefighters emerged, exhausted and looking for water – their clothing powdered with white ash. They said body parts and people clinging to life were strewn among the mountains of concrete, glass, steel, office furniture, and paper.

"It looks like downtown Beirut," firefighter Robbie Rachoi said. "It looks like something that shouldn't have happened here."

Robert James, manager of a sporting goods store near the complex, was in the basement when he heard the explosion. He said he came above ground to see at least five bodies fall from the skyscraper.

"They looked like rag dolls," he said. "It was like the kind of thing you see in movies."

Boris Ozersky, forty-seven, a computer networks analyst, was on the seventieth floor of one of the buildings when he felt an explosion rock it. He raced down seventy flights of stairs. Once outside, amid a crowd in front of a nearby hotel, he said he was trying to calm a panicked woman as the building suddenly collapsed.

"I just got blown somewhere, and then it was total darkness. We tried to get away, but I was blown to the ground. And

I was trying to help this woman, but I couldn't find her in the darkness," Ozersky said. After the dust cleared, he located her.

Throughout lower Manhattan, rescue workers and police officers wore surgical masks to protect them from the dust.

At the city's hospitals hundreds lined up to give blood, after hospital workers yelled on the streets, "Blood donations! Blood donations!"

Firefighter Rudy Weindler, covered in the soot of twelve hours on duty at the wreckage, said he had found only four survivors.

"I lost count of all the dead people I saw," Weindler said. "It is absolutely worse than you could ever imagine."

Thousands upon thousands fled the city, streaming across the Brooklyn and Manhattan bridges on foot, some sobbing, others covered head to toe in gray soot and ashes. With no buses, taxis, or subways, the throng was left with no way home but on foot.

Businessmen walked across the Brooklyn Bridge...their button-down shirts pressed over their faces against the smoke and dust.

Passing cell phones back and forth when the rare call went through, desperate strangers called to each other, "Can you get out?"

A woman pleaded, "Can you call my mother? This is her number."

Another yelled, "How do I get to Queens?"

"Start walking," a police officer yelled back.

# FINANCIAL DISTRICT FILLS WITH SCENES OF HORROR AS TWIN TOWERS COLLAPSE

*By Rachel Donadio, with additional reporting
by Nacha Cattan and Ami Eden
(Jewish Forward staff, September 14, 2001)
Reprinted with permission*

*On Prince Street in Manhattan's stylish SoHo district, more than a mile north of the World Trade Center, you could already smell the smoke. In the distance, great gray billows unfolded above lower Manhattan on a pristine end-of-summer morning.*

By 10 A.M. traffic had thinned to almost nothing outside the boutiques and upscale cosmetics stores on lower Fifth Avenue, just above Washington Square. New Yorkers clogged the sidewalks and looked south, stunned. A lone hot-dog vendor closed up his cart and wheeled it away.

An hour earlier two separate airplanes, hijacked by terrorists, had flown into each of the Twin Towers of the World Trade Center. What began with a thin plume of smoke at 8:48 A.M. had by early afternoon ballooned into the most horrific act of terrorism ever to strike the United States, with thousands feared dead.

In lower Manhattan the fear was reflected in the faces of pedestrians.

When the first tower collapsed, the stunned crowds on Fifth Avenue let out a collective scream. People cried openly. Strangers held each other.

"You can't blame this one on the black man!" shouted a

homeless man as he pushed a shopping cart south down the middle of Fifth Avenue.

"They'll have to put everything underground," a nearby man said. "The markets, the stores. It's the end of New York City."

Near City Hall, about a half-mile east of the World Trade Center, police were herding people aside, pulling them off bicycles, and shouting, "Clear the streets!"

By 10:20 A.M. the tone grew shriller. "It's coming this way!" shouted a police officer on Reade Street, a stone's throw from the old Forward Building, as he herded people northward.

No one knew what exactly was coming where. People exchanged terrified glances. Everyone began moving north.

And then, in the distance, the second tower collapsed.

At Foley Square, the circle of courthouses and federal buildings just above City Hall, the mood was strangely calm. The sun was shining brightly on the plaza, the water plashing in the black marble fountain. Yet every few minutes someone caked in white ash would stumble in. Some stopped to wash their faces in the fountain.

"You have to get it out of your nostrils," a woman in green medical scrubs advised a woman caked in ash who was trying to wipe the dust off her face with a meager tissue.

"There wasn't a lot of crazy panic," said Laura Giordano, caked in ash, as she stood by the fountain and recounted her morning. "I heard everybody yell, 'Run!' " said Ms. Giordano, who works at the World Financial Center, just across the West Side Highway from the Twin Towers. "The police officers just pushed everyone along."

"Tons of cops and firemen are dead," said Jim Whelan, a middle-aged man with a red-striped cotton shirt and a face white from shock. " 'Cause they were on the stairwells going up. We were coming down," he said. "Seventy-seventh floor."

"I felt an explosion," said Mr. Whelan, who said that he worked at John F. Kennedy International Airport but was at the first tower for a meeting. "Stuff came out of the ceiling. I called home. Called my wife to say I was okay." He started to quake. "I gotta go," he said.

Red Cross disaster services ambulances, coated in three inches of white ash, screeched past, sirens wailing. Long lines formed at pay phones. No one's cell phone would work. Passersby leaned into an ABC Television van to try and watch the news feed.

On the corner a street sign read, "Worth Street: Avenue of the Strongest."

Court officers were serving as ad hoc traffic cops. One was fielding questions from passersby wondering when the subways would be running. "We don't know!" he said. "It's the first time it's happened! We don't exactly have a plan!"

A thin row of police stood outside the federal courthouse, awaiting orders. Just months earlier, in that same building, a federal judge had convicted four low-level operatives of Osama bin Laden on charges of carrying out the bombings against the U.S. embassies in Kenya and Tanzania in 1998.

"This'll be like the day they attacked Pearl Harbor," one man said to a police officer.

On Center Street, people began a slow walk north. They chatted with each other, comforted each other.

"Coming in on the 7 train I saw a gaping hole in the World Trade Center," said John Medina, a frightened man in his twenties from Flushing, Queens. "I think we're gonna start fighting someone," he said as he started the long walk to his office on the Upper East Side.

Volunteers were distributing free cups of water, giving traffic information, and offering their office bathrooms. "The E, F, and 7 trains are running," Barbara Olshansky, from the Center for Constitutional Rights, told a worried woman. The center had set up a volunteer table on the sidewalk.

Further north, in midtown Manhattan, ambulances zigzagged through the side streets, avoiding the main thoroughfares to get to New York University Hospital and the Bellevue Hospital Center on First Avenue.

Hordes of New York Police Academy cadets directed traffic. Jeff Valenzana had only been at the academy three months but already commanded an air of authority as he guided taxis and large trucks through the Thirty-third Street and Second Avenue intersection, a block west of the hospitals. "We're closing the whole city down," Valenzana said.

By the early afternoon, a horde of would-be blood donors circled the hospitals. Many were turned away. Igor Shapiro, whose blood type was a rare [form of] O-positive, was not. The twenty-eight-year-old Ukrainian Jewish immigrant said he did not mind waiting two hours to "give something back to this country" to which he came nine years ago.

Menachem Engel, a twenty-seven-year-old analyst at Credit Suisse, didn't bother to get himself checked out as he walked past the desk and exited NYU Medical Center on First

Avenue and Thirty-fourth Street. Mr. Engel could not remember why he had decided to step outside his office at the World Trade Center moments before the first plane crashed into it.

A cloud of debris and smoke had flooded the street, Mr. Engel said, heading straight for him and other pedestrians who fled toward the East River. "It trapped everyone against the water at Wall Street," he said. To escape, he and others moved onto FDR Drive, the scenic highway that rims Manhattan along the East River.

An ambulance of the Hatzalah Orthodox volunteer ambulance corps pulled up to NYU Hospital and delivered two disheveled men holding hard hats who were then wheeled into the emergency room. One, Joe Fuchs, twenty-two, said that he had been working as a volunteer since the first crash, pulling people from the rubble and chaos. "It's crazy," he said. "Everything is just smoky and crazy."

His partner, who identified himself only as Howie, said, "What we've seen — how do you put it in one word? — it's a disaster."

For many, comparisons to the disaster could be found only in Hollywood blockbuster films. "In the movies it happens. It doesn't happen here in the U.S.," said Megan Isaacs, sixteen and a student at the United Nations International School, as she stood on fashionable Lafayette Street in lower Manhattan....

Some were comparing the disaster to the 1996 action movie *Independence Day*, in which several world landmarks including the White House are blown up by aliens.

But if real life was imitating the movies, the movies were

imitating real life – and shutting down. A sign on the door of the United Artists movie theater at Union Square announced that it would be closed until further notice, "due to the extreme emergencies." On the street outside the theater, Army National Guard soldiers in camouflage fatigues were directing traffic on Park Avenue South.

In a newscast, Mayor Rudolph Giuliani said the city should be strong and get on with business.

Behind the smoked glass windows of the posh bar of the W Union Square Hotel, people were drinking martinis.

# CHAPTER FOUR

# Those Who Were Spared

### As told to Sarah Shapiro

*A week later, in shuls throughout the world, the chazzan would intone the awe-inspiring words of U'Nesaneh Tokef, "Who shall live and who shall die?" In those fiery, smoke-filled hours of September 11, thousands saw their own personal miracles, the hashgachah pratis that protected those whose time had not come. Some of the names are fictitious. As much as possible, we have tried to verify the accuracy of the stories. We apologize if there are any errors in details.*

Nachum's brother was in desperate need of a transplant but was unable to raise the required $100,000. Nachum had a friend who worked in the World Trade Center who might be persuaded to give him a loan. The man agreed. He would go to his bank immediately and make arrangements for the money to be transferred, he assured Nachum. While he was gone, the tragedy occurred. After that, he refused to accept repayment. "The money restored two lives," he said.

> > >

Mr. Goodman asked Judy, who worked for him in the World Trade Center, if she would be amenable to a transfer to the company's New Jersey office. Judy knew the move would create a hardship for her. It would consume more time and gasoline and impinge upon family obligations. If she disliked the new workplace, she might have to resign a position she'd held for many years. She felt inclined to refuse. Over the weekend the family weighed the pros and cons. There would be a pay hike and a positive reaction from her employer if she accepted. On the flip side, her failure to comply might foster ill will and jeopardize her job. On Monday, September 10, she presented the boss with a plan: starting tomorrow she would try it out and see how well it worked. On Tuesday morning Judy did not show up at the WTC.

> > >

A few days before September 11, a company located in the World Trade Center closed down, discharging a large number of workers. Devastated, the people were angry at the callous employer who would deprive so many families of their lifeline. Come Tuesday, however, that anger turned into thanksgiving.

> > >

Berel is one of those men who review the entire weekly Torah portion by the end of the week. On the way to work that Tuesday he had almost completed the day's allotment when the train screeched to a halt at his stop. Instead of heading up to his office, he sat down on a bench and completed the verses. His diligence saved his life.

Last summer, for the first time, the Koyfmans sent their daughter to an Orthodox sleep-away camp, where she broke her arm in an accident. Incensed, her parents threatened to sue. The rabbi apologized and advised against taking action. Shortly thereafter, on September 11, when the rabbi learned what had happened at the World Trade Center, and knowing that the girl's father worked there, he called their home to find out if all was well. Her mother told him that her husband had not gone to work that day — he had accompanied his daughter to the hospital to have her cast removed.

Leah stepped out of her apartment that morning to help someone and left her front door open. Assuming Leah forgot to lock it, a well-meaning neighbor did it for her. When Leah returned a few moments later, she could not get back into her house. By the time she found her spare key and collected her handbag and lunch, she had missed the 8:45 train. She would have arrived at the World Trade Center shortly after nine.

$A$fter he finished davening that morning, Feivel realized that his tefillin needed repair, and he resolved to attend to it immediately. When he arrived at the World Trade Center two hours late, he learned that one of the planes had crashed into his floor.

> ➢ ➢ ➢

$O$n Monday, September 10, David, who lives in Israel, donated $1,300 to a synagogue there in honor of his departed father. That night he knew no rest. His mind was in a turmoil. He had already dedicated a new Torah scroll recently to his father's memory. Shouldn't this financial grant be dedicated to something else? On Tuesday morning (Israeli time, before anything had happened in America), he returned to the synagogue and told the rabbi that he wished his donation to be a supplication for the longevity of his children.

At that hour, David's son, who worked at Blue Cross in the World Trade Center, was helping 1,300 employees evacuate the building.

> ➢ ➢ ➢

$W$hen a couple arrived at the airport ten minutes late, the gates had already closed, and no amount of cajoling could get them in. The couple had missed one of the flights that crashed into the towers.

> ➢ ➢ ➢

$E$liezer was boarding the ill-fated plane when he got an

emergency call that his presence was required at an urgent business meeting. He canceled his trip and headed for the Twin Towers, but a traffic jam slowed him down. By the time he arrived, the building was in flames. He was saved twice in one day.

> ➢    ➢    ➢

Cantor Fitzgerald had fired forty *frum* people and gave them their last paycheck that Friday. They went to a *rosh yeshivah* to complain about being fired. He told them they should not view it negatively, because undoubtedly the Creator has a purpose in mind. On Tuesday, over six hundred of their fellow employees were killed.

> ➢    ➢    ➢

On Monday, September 10, a woman who had come to New York from Eretz Yisrael went uptown to shop for her daughter's wedding. After she returned by taxi, she realized she had left her pocketbook containing thousands of dollars, her plane tickets, and passports on the back seat. Two hours later the taxi driver called to tell her he had found it. She asked him to bring it to her, but he said that by the time he finished driving it would be too late. He would meet her the next morning at 8:45 in front of the World Trade Center, where he worked. Afraid that he might forget or change his mind, she and her husband called him back and asked if he would allow them to come to his house in Queens that evening to retrieve the bag. He agreed on condition that they arrive no later than nine-thirty, because he needed to retire early in order to awake in time to go to work. A rabbi drove them there. En route, they lost their way and came a half-hour late, but the taxi driver was still up. The rabbi offered him a substantial reward, but he declined to take it, saying he preferred a blessing. The rabbi wished him a long and happy life. When he awoke late the next morning, he believed the blessing had already been fulfilled.

➤   ➤   ➤

Charlie Dadoon of Deal, New Jersey, whose birthday is September 11, is a *shomer Shabbos* pilot for United Airlines who has demostrated enormous *mesiras nefesh* for *Yiddishkeit*. If United had not decided to fly a different plane for that route, he would have flown one of the hijacked planes.

➤   ➤   ➤

Michael Lomonaco, executive chef of Windows on the World, the restaurant on floors 106 and 107 of Tower One, where about seventy-five of his colleagues were preparing breakfast, missed the attack by five minutes. He had stopped off at an optometrist in the Trade Center's shopping concourse to order reading glasses. The 166 employees and guests who were in the restaurant perished. People who observe kashrus relate that Lomonaco always tried to accommodate religious Jews.

➤   ➤   ➤

A secretary from Monsey, whose father, a prominent rabbi,

had died a few years ago, was in her office at the time of the attack. As she tried to escape, there was an announcement that firefighters were on their way and occupants should remain in their offices. Suddenly she saw the image of her father, who exhorted her to leave immediately, and she made her way out.

Boarding one of the planes that would soon be hijacked, Shmuel realized that he had forgotten to take his tefillin. He would not travel without them, so he got off.

Jake was sitting at his desk on one of the upper floors of the Twin Towers Tuesday morning at eight-thirty when the phone rang. A *meshulach* (fund-raiser) from a yeshivah in Eretz Yisrael was in the lobby and wanted to know if he could come up. Wanting to spare the guest the inconvenience of finding the right bank of elevators and walking past rows of offices in search of him, he told him he would come downstairs. Both were saved.

Sara had applied for a job as a paralegal with a law firm on the eighty-fifth floor of the north tower and with American Express. Although she had all the qualifications, she was not hired. The news hit her hard; she was in urgent need of income. Both firms reported fatalities.

Jack Buchsbaum, chief electrical engineer for the Port Authority of New York and New Jersey, who worked on the seventy-fourth floor of the World Trade Center, said he survived both attacks "because it wasn't my time to go." That Tuesday morning he was in his office having coffee when the first plane struck.

"I looked out the window and saw papers floating in the air. I realized that it wasn't a good sign. From my experience of the previous bombing, when I was on the seventy-second floor, I knew to head for the stairs. The trip down was slow, but everyone was calm. As soon as we found out what had happened, I said it was a terrorist attack, that it was Osama bin Laden, and that the hijackers were pilots. I was right about that. But I kept assuring people that the building wouldn't fall because it was designed to resist attack by a plane. I guess I was wrong about that."

As in 1993, Buchsbaum walked to safety and found his way home.

Hennie, a teacher, had called a repairman to fix her air conditioner. He could only be at her house at 9 A.M. on that Tuesday, but she had to be in school at that time. She asked her husband, Gerald, if he could be a little late for work. He said he had an important meeting, but he would wait until nine. The repairman arrived on time but found the air conditioner needed no repair. Gerald paid the fee and ran for the train. When he exited the subway, he saw his building in flames.

Bernard Kesselman, fifty-six, who lives in Long Island, worked as an attorney for Aon Corporation, the country's second largest insurance brokerage firm, on the hundredth floor of the World Trade Center. On Monday, he told his secretary that he would be in very early the next morning, because he had a lot of work to do. Exhausted, he retired at 7:30 P.M., expecting to awake in time for Selichos and davening. He took the 7:38 Long Island Railroad train, which normally got him to the office at 8:45. The train, usually punctual, was twenty-five minutes late. When he arrived in Manhattan, he saw both towers on fire. In an effort to determine the whereabouts of his coworkers, he began to scour the area. The buildings meanwhile collapsed.

"This huge cloud of dirt and bricks was coming at me," he said. "The people in front of me ran and fell, and I fell near them. I happened to fall under an iron scaffold. Some of the falling bricks were hitting the scaffold. When the cloud hit me, there was complete blackness. I couldn't see or breathe. I was choking and spitting. When the bricks stopped falling, I got up and started walking toward the East River. There was a howling wind. I thought, *This is what Gehinnom must be like.* It was very weird. I was taking little baby steps in order not to trip. You couldn't see where you were walking." A car service brought him to safety.

Two hundred of the New York firm's one thousand employees perished.

O n Monday night thunderstorms caused delays in landings at various airports, including New York's JFK, which, in turn, caused delays in other flights en route to New York.

That's why Zvi Feldman arrived in Manhattan from Denver two hours later than planned. He was supposed to have arrived at six on Tuesday morning, long before his associate would report to work at the World Trade Center. He decided he would wait on an observation deck near the top of the building before heading for his associate's office.

But he arrived in New York after eight, hopped in a cab to downtown Manhattan, and was on the Midtown Bridge when the north tower imploded. Though the radio announced that a small plane had struck the building, it did not deter him from proceeding onward.

A few blocks from his destination, gnarled traffic made him decide to get out and walk. It was about 9 A.M., and he heard another explosion. He looked up and saw the fireball created by the second implosion. Suddenly people realized it was an attack. There was screaming, running, and crying.

Zvi and several other Orthodox men took shelter in an electronics store operated by Arab Americans. Recalling the shoes and family photographs in the wreckage and the fear and panic on people's faces, he said the devastation and destruction were indescribable. Yet there was so much *chessed*: storekeepers opening their doors to take in people off the street, shoe stores giving out free athletic shoes to women who could not navigate in high heels, Hatzalah members (whom he joined) doling out water to firefighters and emergency workers, firefighters risking their lives to save people.

As an Orthodox Jew, he believes the thunderstorms and the plane delays were part of the Creator's master plan to save his life and the lives of thousands of others. He said the most difficult part was being able to thank Him for sparing his life.

➤    ➤    ➤

*Tzvi Hersh, a former vice president of Lehman Brothers and, most recently, director of data services at Meta Matrix, Inc., relates:*

I am in the information technology field. My expertise is in real-time delivery of market data information from the stock exchanges to financial institutions.

I had received an e-mail inviting me to a September 11 Risk-Waters seminar to be held on the 106th floor of the north tower of the World Trade Center, in Windows on the World. It said that the program would begin at 8:00 A.M., the chairman's opening remarks at 8:30, and the first speaker was scheduled to start at 8:40.

When I first received the invitation a month before the event, I discarded it, because this year's fee was not worth it. I would have loved to go, since I would have been able to network with other members of my profession.

On September 10, I received an e-mail saying that they were extending a gratis invitation to some of the people who had come to previous seminars — they had ten openings available for the first respondents. Without batting an eyelash, I answered that it would be my pleasure to attend.

As soon as I sent off my reply, I realized that on that same day I had a 4:30 appointment in Lakewood, where I live, but I figured I would go early to the Manhattan event and then take the two o'clock bus back to Lakewood.

That night I prepared my bus tickets, laid out my clothing, and set my alarm clock for 5:30 A.M. I planned to leave at 6:30. My wife, who had her own plans, rose a half-hour earlier. Her moving around in the room woke me, and I was upset that I had lost a half-hour's sleep. But I consoled myself thinking, *Why am I so annoyed? There's plenty of time until the four-thirty appointment. I will go to shul and then come back and take a nap.* I completely forgot about the seminar at the Twin Towers.

At about nine in the morning, my son phoned me from Brooklyn to tell me what was happening. My sister called from Boston at 9:10, alarmed, reminding me that I was supposed to be at the meeting. I replied, "I missed the meeting!" Then I said, "Thank God, I missed the meeting!"

All eighty-three people who were at the seminar perished along with most of the entire staff of Windows on the World. One hundred forty-three people who were scheduled to attend the seminar had not arrived. I was one of them.

➣   ➣   ➣

Yankel gave a *meshulach* from Eretz Yisrael a ride to lower Manhattan. Arriving at the World Trade Center parking lot, he told the guest which way to go to his destination, excusing himself for not taking him and explaining that he feared he would be late for work. The Israeli said he would not be able to find his way alone and begged Yankel to drop him off. Yankel complied and lived to tell the story.

Shimon would be late for work, but he couldn't leave his friend's son's bris until it was over. And then it was all over.

Neil, thirty-three, a legal assistant, was angry with himself when he twisted his ankle while hiking during a vacation in Maine. Because of this, he missed his Tuesday morning trip home to Los Angeles from Boston on the American Airlines flight that was hijacked and crashed into the World Trade Center.

An attorney used to pick up his friend Joe, an employee of Cantor Fitzgerald, every Tuesday morning, and they would drive to a 9 A.M. Torah lecture together. Every Monday night he e-mailed Joe to remind him to be ready. The understanding was that if Joe was not there when he came by at 7:30, he would leave without him rather than risk being late for work. Even though Joe had not responded this time, the attorney drove to his house and waited outside for ten minutes. Joe finally came out, and they were on their way. While they were at the lecture, more than six hundred employees at Cantor Fitzgerald went to their death.

Boris, the owner of several elegant mansions and luxury cars, was driving in the Battery Tunnel that Tuesday morning when the tunnel became enveloped in smoke. Someone advised him to remove his shirt and place it over his mouth. Boris commented that he could buy anything his heart desired, yet that which was free, a breath of fresh air, was unattainable.

# CHAPTER FIVE

# Those Who Were Saved

## DAVID'S STORY

*By David Frank*
*Reprinted with permission*

*I was on my way to the World Trade Center. I had made it to the parking lot on time, at about 7:50 A.M., and parked in the Edison parking lot just across the street from Tower Two. This was my second time in the lot; I had visited our Quantum | ATL Solution Center about two months ago to meet with Mike Hingson, our ATL VAR territory manager.*

After picking up my parking stub, I lugged my computer bag up the street, past the Marriott to Tower One. Upon entering the building, I realized my roadrunner portfolio was back in the car. So back I went to the lot, found the car (the lot was virtually empty – curious), and scooped up the portfolio.

I remember looking up at Tower Two. Just looking up. It was an absolutely perfect day. Cloudless. High sixties, low seventies. The air windswept and free. I walked back to Tower One. I remember thinking how heavy the bag was and how excited I was about the Solution Center event with my Ingram associates. Joe Santoro, my manager and friend, would arrive at around nine.

I got to the Security Center and an attendant was able to help me right away. But the attendant just couldn't get hold of Mike Hingson. Finally I got out my cell phone and was able to reach him. Just as I was being processed, our friends from Ingram showed up: Todd Riley, Mark McClure, Patrick Dempsey, Sheri Leach, Amy Phillips, Lisa Amatura, and Jason Hernandez.

As I write this, I have no idea if these people are alive.

We all got processed, then caught a ride. Mark led the way to the Solutions Center but let me go in first.

It was 8:25.

The Quantum|ATL suite was located on the seventy-eighth floor of Tower One. When you entered the suite, a series of four rooms ran along the south side of the tower. The Trade Center's windows were tall and very narrow, perhaps only a foot wide. Looking out required a deliberate move toward the window. The viewer was rewarded with a spectacular view of New York Harbor and the Statue of Liberty. Pure Americana!

I realized it would not be preferable to have our guests go through a security check during the actual training sessions, so I went back downstairs and met with the head of Security for the day. He showed me a way to fax down an attendee list so that when guests arrived at Security they wouldn't have to call up each time. I got the instructions and went back upstairs. Just before going downstairs to see the security manager, the thought that the World Trade Center was a "target" ran through my mind. I went back into the suite and began to compose the fax.

Todd helped out with the list. I needed to put it all on the company letterhead in accordance with Security's instruction. After composing the fax, I realized that the address on Mike's letterhead to was One Liberty. I asked Mike if he had any WTC letterheads. Mike and I went back to his office, leaving the Ingram folks split between the conference room and the extra room with food. He approached the bookcase and rummaged around a bit and then moved away toward his desk. I looked again but didn't find what I needed and turned back to Mike. He was about ten feet from one of the windows.

Our lives changed forever at 8:45.

The explosion rocked the entire structure. Instantly, the windows just above us blew, and debris on fire tumbled past along with tens of thousands of pieces of printer paper. I thought, *Confetti.* The noise was bright, metallic, deafening. The building groaned and leaned south dramatically in slow motion. Would the structure hold?

I braced myself with my feet to keep from sliding. Then back we went in reverse. This time I braced myself with my hands. At this point I don't remember if we went back and forth again, but I do remember that the swaying stopped, and, to my dismay, the structure sunk downward. Was it a terrorist attack? *No. Probably an explosion in an office above due to a gas leak. But it's too intense for that. But why would they attack the top of the tower?* The building shuttered to a stop.

I think it was Amy Phillips from Ingram who ran into Mike's office, looked out the window, and ran out. Mike moved to his desk and immediately got on the phone to his wife. I ran to find the Ingram people.

A smell of what I thought was gasoline filled the air. I opened the suite door to the hallway to see all the Ingram people huddled together. Lights overhead were out, building and ceiling materials on the floor. There was a light on at the end of the corridor.

Mark McClure looked at me with terror-filled eyes. I pointed down the corridor and yelled, "Go!" I ran back into the suite and to Mike's office. I went to the window, not without fear, wondering...and looked up.

Just above was a roar of orange light, black smoke, multi-colored paper flying, burnt cinders accenting the sky, and that smell of gas. Then my gaze fell on Tower Two. I observed a large black hole rimmed with fire and smoke. Only later Wednesday night did I understand that this was collateral damage from the explosion in Tower One. In spite of my emotional reaction to what was happening, my mind focused like a laser beam and I knew what I had to do. I turned to Mike and yelled, "We have to get out! Now!"

But we didn't leave immediately. We gathered our things. I grabbed my computer bag by the handle and portfolio with the other hand. Mike strapped on his computer bag and reached for his beautiful yellow Lab guide dog, Roselle.

We got to the door, and I said, "Mike, you know they will not let you up here, whether it's a terrorist attack or some kind of accident, for a very long time. Shouldn't we turn off the equipment?"

Mike agreed. So back in we went looking for the Off switch. I went to the back of the P3000, saw the cables, but in the confusion I could not for the life of me find the outlet to pull the plug! Mike had no luck with the front of the machines. So we abandoned the idea. We used up about thirty seconds.

We turned into the hallway corridor and headed for the elevator in the central corridor. I was immediately concerned. The smoke was heavy and filled with gas (jet fuel). We made it to the central elevator corridor. Not for a moment did we think the elevators were working.

Lots of confusion. Lots of smoke. Lots of sunlight from the east window wall illuminating both. A white-shirted WTC employee and a man in a utility uniform were running around with rags over their mouths. I noticed that the inch-thick dark green marble lining the elevator bank's walls had buckled and snapped. Major structural damage. They wouldn't let anyone in here for a very long time.

Someone mentioned that the stairwell was not passable. How would we get down? The man in the dark utility suit went to the stairwell and opened the door. Away we went on a seventy-eight-floor journey down a well-lit stairway clear of debris, escaping from the terrible fire above.

It was about 8:55.

Mike had me get in front of him, Roselle to his left. The first twenty or so floors went smoothly. No one was in front of us! Just a few people in back. They were patient, but we obviously slowed them down, so we let them pass. If I remember correctly, around the high forties, low fifties, we hit a traffic jam of people in the stairwell. I looked down. Hundreds of heads and feet were below us. This was not good. And yet we were very calm, and all the people in the stairwell were well behaved.

Should we exit onto another floor? The fire was above and could work itself lower. But what if the stairwell filled with smoke and gas? Where else could we go? Only down! Several people in line were clearly panicked, sobbing, but staying in place. Others saw Mike and Roselle, asked if I was with them, and began to call for others below to "move right" to make room for us to come down. No one complained. What generosity of spirit!

Mike had his radio on, and others mentioned that a plane had hit our building. That maybe there were two planes. That would explain what I had seen. So it was jet fuel, after all. We certainly had inhaled a lot of it! Around the mid-forties, I think, we heard voices from above yelling, "Move right. Burn victims coming down!"

I caught my first glimpse of her on the staircase above me. She was in her late twenties, early thirties. She turned the corner toward us. Two or three people behind her. She walked like a zombie. Eyes straight ahead. Expressionless. Clothes burned off of half her body. Third-degree burns. Skin falling off her arms, neck, and face. Her blonde hair caked in gray slime. Fully ambulatory. Totally in shock. What appreciation I have for shock now!

About fifteen minutes later a second woman came down. It was bizarre. She was almost the same age, with the same height, weight, hair color, burns, emotionless expression.

Shock. As we got into the low forties, the reek of the jet fuel got much more intense. I thought we might pass out. People were clearly suffering the intense fumes, and others were clearly beginning to panic. Roselle was not doing well, panting heavily, and we all needed water.

Some people began passing small Poland Spring water bottles up to us from the floor below. This was a real relief. Roselle loved it. It cut some of the fuel taste burning our throats. It eased our sense of dehydration and smoke inhalation.

I opened the door to the forties floor, and we stood in the doorway momentarily. I looked and saw no one on the floor. There was only smoke and the smell of more jet fuel. We kept to the stairway.

Today I believe that when the aircraft hit the north face of the tower, its momentum, driven by the aircraft structure and fuel, vivisected the floor, slicing through the elevator shaft and effectively dumping fuel from the low nineties all the way down to the bottom. That's why we kept smelling fuel almost all the way down.

Around the forties, or maybe it was the high thirties, we ran into our first real hero. A New York City fireman. He was coming up, walking from the lobby on his way to the low nineties, clothed in a heavy fireman's hat, fire-retardant thigh-length jacket, and similar pants (called "bunker gear"), yellow glow strips around the biceps, thighs, and hat. Heavy gloves. They were carrying an unbelievable array of equipment: axes, picks, shovels, fire hoses, and oxygen tanks. It must have been in excess of seventy-five pounds per man including clothing.

Unbelievable! They were perspiring profusely, exhausted. And they had to go all the way to the nineties!

This was not lost on the crowd. We all broke out in applause at one point. It was a wonderful moment. Mike and I patted many on the back with a "God bless you." Extremely polite, constantly inquiring about our welfare. "Are you all right?" to Mike. Mike: "I'm fine, thank you." Fireman: "Are you with this guy?" pointing to Mike. Me: "Yes, I'm with Mike, and we are okay, thank you." We had this conversation with virtually everyone of the thirty-five or forty firemen who passed us. They are all gone now. We cannot praise them enough.

We finally got to the second floor. It must have been around 9:35 or 9:40. Water was on the landing. I cautioned Mike. Roselle loved it — she drank right from the floor, and it perked her up. She was going to need the energy. When we got down to the very last landing, water had accumulated in the stairwell.

We exited the stairwell into the lobby. It was a war zone. I know this is an overused phrase, but it really fit. There were debris — wall material, ceiling tiles, paper, garbage — in a lake of water an ankle deep. In front of us was a torrential rainfall over the exit turnstiles. I alerted Mike that he was about to get very wet but that there was no other danger.

We went through the turnstiles. Police and WTC personnel in white shirts, black pants, and security badges kept yelling, gesturing, "Keep moving!"

We moved through the eastern exit doors of Tower One into the indoor mall that connected the two towers. More water and lots of noise! Left now and heading north. "Keep moving!" Lights were on. Up some stairs. Down a dark narrow corridor. Light at the end. The sky! We were out!

We had exited the northeast corner of the entire complex. There were medical personnel coming at us. "We're fine. No injuries here. Thank you!"

Television people moved forward to ask questions, but we were moving and did not want to stop. They didn't press it (no pun intended). Mike said, "David, you did well today." It was nice to hear.

Just about thirty yards outside the exit, I turned and looked up over my right shoulder and witnessed what I thought was the most monstrous sight of my life: both towers ringed by fire around their perimeters, flames sharp and lapping at steel, a huge plume from Tower One joining up with Tower Two, creating a river of gray black smoke against a perfectly blue sky.

We had to keep moving. We crossed the street and began to amble south on Broadway. I was thinking about transportation and that maybe there was a way to get back south near Tower Two to get the rental car and my stuff and provide transportation for Mike and myself.

This immediately showed itself to be a very bad idea, so we just stopped on Broadway. There were a dozens of people on Broadway going both ways. The police didn't have the street blocked to foot traffic. I decided to pull out my DV camera and take a quick shot of our tower. I pointed the camera and ran it for about five seconds. I couldn't get both towers due to a building blocking my view of Tower Two, but I got ours. Then I said to Mike that we had to get out of there.

I put the camera in my bag and stood up. Then we heard a very distinctive and unforgettable sound. Tower Two was coming down. The sound was like a subway train, with metal poles snapping in two. Add in a chorus of screams and you get the picture. Not to mention the three-hundred-foot-tall debris cloud coming at us at high speed. Not to mention that the building was tall enough to fall on us if it fell our way. (We learned later that this was partially true.) We ran for our lives.

Quickly I galloped around the corner, heading east, and then I realized that I had left Mike behind. Four leaps back and I grabbed him. We ducked into a subway-type entrance just as the cloud engulfed us. The street went completely black. I mean black. There was absolutely no light at all. But there was light in this little entrance.

It turned out to be a mini-mall underneath the street, connected, Mike later heard, to the subway system. However, even though my reaction to go toward the light was natural, I thought I had made a fatal error. The cloud had filled the stairwell going down instantly. What if the cloud kept filling the mall and we had no ventilation? If we had stayed above on the street, would the air be clearing faster and give us a chance to breathe?

I couldn't see Mike in front of me. I knew he was a foot away, but I couldn't see him. Couldn't see Roselle. Couldn't see my feet. Nostrils filling up fast with concrete ash. "Breath shallow!"

A completely unique feeling entered my mind. I was going to die today with Mike Hingson. Everyone dies and this was our time. I told Mike, "I don't think we're going to make it,

Mike." It was, I know now, an apology. I felt that I had made the wrong choice.

We kept going down. We heard people asking for help. We couldn't see them even with the lights on. We shuffled on. I saw another staircase ahead about ten feet away. I went for it. It was blocked by a security gate. No way to go further. But a little fresh air was coming up! I kneeled to get closer and told Mike to do the same. He remained standing. Roselle was caked and panting heavily.

Then an angel appeared. His name was Lou. No dust on Lou! Just a mask. "Go down this hallway and into the room at the end. You'll be all right in there." Sure enough, it turned out that Lou was some kind of janitor (angel) and had been in this little six-by-twenty-foot locker room with a water fountain and a fan! One of the victims was vomiting badly over the fountain. Another woman came in, caked in ash, terrified. I shook her a little and got her name. Cheryl. She calmed down, and the man at the fountain seemed to recover a bit.

Mike and I both got to the fountain. The police showed up about seven minutes later, demanding that we leave and go back upstairs. The density of the cloud, even below ground, had diminished enough so we could see about fifteen feet ahead, so we were able to get back to the top. We had gone down three levels! We never saw Lou again.

Up on the street we were still in the cloud but could see light to the east. What an eerie view. Darkness behind us, light at the end of the tunnel cloud. We were caked and filled with gunk but kept walking. Finally the cloud eased up, and we could see City Hall to the north.

We found a pay phone. It worked! Somewhat. I think this is when I called my sister Claire in Stonybrook, my wife Jennifer, and my friend Hugh on the Upper West Side. Mike was having some luck with his phone, too. We kept walking to the northeast down an empty street. I decided to steer us away from City Hall and go further east. More sights: an ambulance emerging from the cloud down by the WTC and spilling ash along the way; an abandoned food cart – the fruit, soda cans, bottled water, all dusted with ash; an inch of ash covering the street. Mike wanted to get to a restaurant to sit down and rest. We headed for Chinatown. We approached the Brooklyn Bridge and saw throngs of people on foot walking to Brooklyn. Some walking into the chaos (Manhattan) – looking for loved ones, colleagues? Orderly, quiet. An overwhelming sight.

On the way to the Manhattan Bridge area, we heard our tower begin to fall. The sound was unmistakable. To my horror, another large debris cloud was racing our way. This time I grabbed Mike by the arm, and we ran as best we could to safety. The edge of the cloud missed us by fifty yards. No way were we going to go through that again!

Then the Manhattan Bridge. Same as the Brooklyn. The approaches were really the border of the emergency zone. Anything south of Canal Street was off limits. Throngs of people again on foot. Massive traffic jam but no horns.

We crossed Canal, found a wonderful little square with a bench to rest. Then on to a restaurant where we hung out for two hours. We got more phone calls done. I wanted to ensure that Mike had a bed for the night because we didn't think the bridges and tunnels would be open and we wouldn't be able to get home. All throughout our walk after escaping the first debris cloud, we were approached by all kinds of people. "You are blessed." "God gave you a gift." "You've been reborn." "You've been extraordinarily lucky." Mike and I agreed.

We hitched a ride and then walked a while and then caught a bus. All transportation was free. We got to Thirty-second Street and Sixth Avenue and walked the one block to Penn Station. The streets were full and so quiet. Looking downtown, I saw the plume. No towers. Just a huge cloud. We moved onward to New Jersey Transit. Again, throngs of orderly, quiet people. The trains were running free and without schedule. A train pulled into the station. They loaded it up and sent it on its way.

I got Mike and Roselle to the head of the line and away. He went, apparently with minimal discomfort, off to his family. I walked to the subway and caught the number 1 to 116th Street and my dear friend's on the Upper West Side. For the first time I saw the pictures...all through the night....

Mike and I (and Roselle) had been blessed with the opportunity to live another day and gain strength from extraordinary adversity. We will recover, but we will never be the same. Mike and I helped each other, and we were helped by complete strangers and dear friends. We survived with a sense of dignity, even humor, but we are not untouched. You know. Life is short. Don't waste it.

I found out that our friends from Ingram were alive and well early Wednesday morning. What a relief! Joe Santoro ended up where I believed (and prayed) he would — about ten blocks north of the towers on Fourteenth Street. Joe has already lost one fireman friend to the tragedy. Let's hope that's the end of it.

*Roselle is a three-year-old Seeing-Eye dog.*
*Mike Hingson, fifty-one, has been blind since birth.*

## ESCAPING DEATH TWICE

*Ari left the house ten minutes later than usual after helping his son with his homework. His office at Cantor Fitzgerald was on the 101st floor, and he had to change at the seventy-eighth for a second elevator. As he was waiting, he heard a volcanic explosion.*

The building caught on fire. The electricity went off. He followed a small light to an office and went in. The fire warden showed people to the emergency steps, and about fifteen people began walking down. A coworker, Virginia, was hurt and pleaded with him not to leave her stranded. He said he would try to see her to safety. The cell phones all went dead, and he could not call for help. But, by some miracle, his wife was able to get through. He told her he was all right. After that, the phone was inoperable again.

Virginia was losing strength, but he encouraged her to be strong. At the bottom of the steps police directed them, and he found someone to help Virginia. He could not understand why the second building was also on fire until someone said that two planes had crashed into the two buildings.

Virginia was put into the first ambulance out, and Ari went along. As soon as they arrived at the hospital, he heard that the second building had collapsed. Ari was thankful he had gone with her; if he had stayed he might have been a casualty.

Lying in her hospital bed swathed in bandages, Virginia, forty-four, watched the account of what she had missed on TV. Of the one thousand people employed at Cantor Fitzgerald's World Trade office, about 370 were not at work when the first plane hit the north tower. Of the 630 who were there, almost all died. Her survival was a miracle, she knew.

An audit director, she usually left for work at 7 A.M. and arrived at her office between eight and eight-thirty. On that Tuesday, her two dogs had refused to come inside, and she could not leave home until they did. She settled in with a second cup of coffee to wait for them and left later.

By 8:35 she was in the lobby of the north tower waiting what seemed like forever for the elevator. Two of them were being repaired, and the others were running slow. When one finally opened its doors, Virginia packed in and got off at the seventy-eighth floor to take the second elevator to the 101st floor. When the doors opened, the passengers heard a deafening explosion, they were faced with a wall of fire.

Virginia decided to dash through the flames rather than remain in the elevator. When she got through, she was aflame, her hair and clothing on fire. She dropped to the ground and rolled over and over, putting out the flames. But her skin was so burnt that her face, hands, and arms were no longer recognizable. She saw Ari and asked him for help. They took the stairs.

People who knew her screamed when they saw her. With Ari's encouragement, she made it to the ground floor and out of the building. A few minutes later, after the ambulance pulled away, the first tower fell. She had escaped death for the second time that morning.

# THE DARK CLOUD

*As told to Sorah Shapiro*

*Doug's apartment was one block south of the World Trade Center. He was home when the first tower was hit, and he went out into the street to search for his brother, who worked on the ninety-eighth floor. (His brother was late for work that morning and survived!) Suddenly he felt the rumblings of the first tower beginning to fall.*

He said it was like nothing he had ever felt or seen before. The building began to move; it seemed unreal, like a cartoon. Then it came crashing to the ground. Doug ran. Doug is an athlete, and his legs served him well. But the smoke and debris were faster than he was. The billowing smoke was brown and black. As the dust and smoke and debris overtook him, a hand reached out and pulled him into an open parking garage. There were others there already. Almost instantly the garage filled with dust and soot; the day instantly turned into night. Doug could see nothing. Nothing. People were screaming and choking. Doug said he was sure he was going to die. He couldn't breathe, and instinctively he felt he had to get out of there.

He called out to people he couldn't see and got them together, and they made their way out, hand in hand. The street was filled with people, some dazed and bleeding, some screaming. He knew he had to get back to his apartment (if it was still standing) and try to rescue his wife, Amy, who was still there. Choking and coughing, his face pelted with the still falling tiny shards of glass and bits of the fallen building, he put his hand up to shield his face and slowly made his way back toward his apartment. He had no way of knowing what he might find.

Miraculously his building was still standing. When he went in, it was eerily silent. He called out. Amy called back. She was alive and upstairs in their apartment, where several other tenants and a FedEx man had taken refuge. They had been watching the TV coverage when they saw the tower begin to fall and then the screen went dark.

Inside the apartment it was like someone had turned out all the lights. It was nearly completely dark, the windows covered with a thick coat of the falling soot. He told them they had to get out; it wasn't safe. He led them out, and they all began to walk toward the water when the unthinkable happened. The horribly familiar rumble began again. The second tower was coming down. Everyone ran for their lives.

# TWO-TIME SURVIVOR
*By Sorah Shapiro*

*Blank spaces stare back at Norma as she strains her eyes on the Manhattan skyline from her balcony in Rockaway Beach. One of them, One World Trade Center, was her workplace. Having emerged unscathed from that building twice in eight years, hers is not only a story of the Twin Towers but of twin survivals.*

Recounting the miracles from her tenth-floor apartment one recent afternoon, her gaze was fixed on a small, frail girl sitting in a wheelchair in the center of her living room. It was surely to care for her nine-year-old grandchild Danielle, who herself had virtually risen from the grave, that she stared down death twice, she believes.

It happened in the summer of 1996. Norma received word that Danielle, who had been wading in the children's pool, had drowned. Pronounced dead on arrival at the hospital, the child was finally resuscitated but remained permanently brain damaged. Her mother, Norma's daughter, had recently remarried, and the responsibility for caring for the child, who would no longer speak or walk and would require diapering and feeding through a gastric tube, rested with Norma.

"I truly believe that the reason I remained alive was to help my daughter look after Danielle. She may be nine, but she's like an eight-month-old baby. It's an arduous task, and it would have been too much for my daughter to handle," she says.

On this day, September 11, Norma, fifty-six and a public information officer for the New York Metropolitan Transportation Council, was sitting at her desk on the eighty-second floor when she heard a thunderous jolt.

"We looked out the window and saw a fireball and debris raining down. The building did not shake. It tilted momentarily and sprang back as if bowing its head to us and saying, 'I'm giving you a chance to get out. Do it now!'"

Someone in the office, whom Norma refers to as one of the angels who saved her, issued a clarion call to evacuate. "Get out! Get out now!" he screamed. After a mass exodus from the office, she and about twenty-five coworkers embarked on a one-hour trek down the narrow staircase single file. Three stayed behind.

"One was running around answering the phones. Another had hurt his leg and was waiting for the rescue workers. The third was probably working in his office. We found out later that we lost them."

On her way out, Norma decided to return to the office to retrieve her handbag, which contained $650. Though the halls were enfolded with black smoke, she groped her way back to the stairwell in the dark.

Normally she would not have been able to navigate the eighty-two flights due to her arthritic knees. But luck had it that the night before, when throbbing pain robbed her of sleep, she wrapped her knees in magnets and awoke the next morning pain-free and euphoric.

"I was so happy. I just couldn't believe I could flex my knees. An angel must have been preparing me for what lay ahead."

"As we walked down," she continues, "we were joking and laughing. We didn't know the severity of what happened. When we got about midway, we found out that a hijacked jetliner had plunged into the ninety-sixth floor of our building. A few young ladies were getting hysterical. I took one by the shoulder and said, 'Take a deep breath and calm down. I've been through this before, and this is a piece of cake compared to last time. Just take it easy, and we'll all be okay.' "

As they were descending the steps, young firefighters,

some breathless or on the verge of collapse, were ascending, armed with heavy equipment.

"Some were radioing for help. Others were opening doors to go into offices and wait for help. *Such young kids*, I thought. I began to feel exhausted. A fireman offered me water, but I said, 'No, thank you. Keep the water. I'm leaving, but you're just arriving. You'll be needing it more than I.' I wished him luck. I'll never forget those young eyes that looked into mine and said, 'Thank you, miss.' "

When she reached the concourse, water from the sprinkler system was gushing in every direction, and it was slippery underfoot. Someone was shouting, "Hurry up! Do not look to the left!" But like the biblical wife of Lot escaping a burning Sodom, Norma did look, and what she saw will haunt her forever.

"I saw the severed head of a white male, with no shoulders or neck, just sitting straight up, looking at me, two burned legs in burned sneakers, a fully dressed torso, and chunks of body parts strewn all over the place. I began to scream. The EMS tagged me around my neck and dragged me across the street. They wanted to give me oxygen.

"I had only been out of the building about ten minutes when suddenly I heard this low, rumbling sound. When I looked around, the building was coming down. It looked like a huge cloud of crushed-up cement, like a big ball of dirt."

People were shrieking and running and trampling one another. Observing a man pressing his body against the side entrance of a hotel, she did the same. Then there was utter darkness and silence. She felt as if pulverized glass was cutting her throat. Her eyes and skin were burning from the falling debris. She waited.

"The man said to me, 'Lady, give me your hand, and don't let go!' I took his hand, and he pulled me for three or four blocks. We came to an abandoned cart. He passed me some juice and water and told me to wash my eyes and drink. He pointed me to a hospital and then turned his back and walked away. That was an angel sent to save me."

In the hospital ladies' room, Norma doused her head in the sink, washed her jacket and dress, and put them back on again, wet. Wandering through the hallways, she encountered two coworkers. They hugged one another, cried, and shared their stories, then decided to head home. When they reached the edge of the Brooklyn Bridge by foot, an emergency vehicle picked them up and hauled them across. Then a special bus brought them to Brighton Beach. It was close to 3 P.M. when her cell phone finally allowed her to dial out. She learned that her son had left his job in Brooklyn in search of her. Someone took pity and delivered her to Rockaway Beach, where she was reunited with her family.

"People just couldn't believe I got out of the building alive, considering I was pretty much disabled because of my knees. You see, the good angels looked after me," she says with a smile.

Although the recent attack was of greater magnitude than that of 1993, Norma says this time her escape was much easier. But both times she was "assisted by angels."

"At least we had light this time, and there was no smoke in the staircase, but in 1993 we felt our way down in pitch darkness and a cloud of smoke. Every now and then someone flicked a cigarette lighter or struck a match, but for the most part it was totally black. If not for those angels, I would never have lived through either attack."

She was one of the ten in her office who survived both attacks.

Norma shifted her glance to Danielle, who was laughing and crying. Both seemed happy for the miracles but saddened that life would never be the same.

# CHAPTER SIX

# Hatzalah

*"Hatzalah was the most well-organized organization at the scene," said Rabbi Edgar Gluck when receiving an award at a charity function in New Jersey three months after that day. "We had about 250 vehicles, 350 volunteers, and forty ambulances. Our members came from all over New York State. The head of the EMS for New York City, Chief Robert McCracken, came over to us and asked how many fatalities we had. We said, 'None.' 'How many people missing?' 'None.' 'How many injured?' 'About three.' He pointed heavenward and said, 'He is watching over you people.' He didn't believe it."*

## FROM RESCUER TO RESCUED
## A Firsthand Account

By Hatzalah member Shaya Goldstein
(Country Yossie Magazine, November 2001)
Reprinted with permission

*I write this with thanks to God that I am able to write it and not be written about!*

As we were dispatched to the Twin Towers for a fire, not knowing what we were getting into, I rode in the Hatzalah ambulance to Manhattan. We were able to clearly see the upper portion of the towers on fire from the Prospect Expressway on the way into the Battery Tunnel.

As we got out of the tunnel and turned onto West Street, I saw body parts all over the street. I saw a part of the airplane. It looked like an engine behind a burned car. As we got closer, we were told to park the ambulance right near the towers. I think we were originally right behind the towers. Then there was a report that a third plane might be coming into the buildings, so we got back in the ambulance and started to drive a little further away. Then we were told it was all clear and that we should park the ambulance on the street behind the towers.

We were parked and waiting for directions from the command center, which was being set up in the lobby of the towers. While we were waiting, a lot of Hatzalah members gathered near the ambulances, watching the towers burn. All that there was between the towers and us was one building. As we waited, we started to see people jumping out of the windows of the towers below the fire floors. Their choice was frying in the building or jumping to their deaths. It was a sight I don't think I will ever forget. We just started to say *tehillim*. How helpless we all felt knowing that there was nothing we could do besides watching them fall to their deaths.

As we were waiting for instructions, we heard a loud rumble. I looked up and saw one of the towers starting to come straight down on itself. I, along with everyone else, ran for my life. About half a block down there was a tremendous cloud of smoke, dust, and debris that had caught up with us. At that point it became dark, so dark you couldn't see an inch in front of you. The smoke and debris were so thick that I was not able to breathe. I can only compare it to putting a vacuum cleaner bag full of dust over your head and trying to see and breathe with it on. It was impossible to keep my eyes open; they were burning from everything in the air. As I was running, I started to get very short of breath. The air was so thick you could cut it! It was like the plague of darkness.

As we were running, another Hatzalah member tripped. I stopped to help him get up. Thank God, he was able to get up. I think he would have been stampeded by all the masses of people running. At the same time, I noticed a two-way radio on the floor. In all the chaos, for some reason I picked it up. About half a block down, the smoke and debris caught up to us. We couldn't see a thing nor were we able to breathe. I knew that I had to find shelter somehow, not knowing what was coming off the tower or how far it was flying. I considered hiding under a fire truck, but it was getting hard to breathe.

I was getting out of breath and knew I had to get into a building. I ran into an alleyway and stopped running. It was getting very hard to breathe, and I was breathing very fast from running. I sat down and thought to myself that this was probably going to be the end! I figured if I kept running I would definitely not survive. I would need too much oxygen, and there wasn't much.

I knew there was a building somewhere in this courtyard. I just had to calm down and find a window to break and climb in. At this point, I heard people yelling if anybody was around, and I answered. We were still unable to see a thing. It was so quiet; there was not a sound. Some big guy tripped on me while I was sitting, trying to calm down. He asked if I am a person. I told him to hold on to me and together we would survive. We held on to each other and felt our way to a wall of a building. We were able to feel a big window and then followed it, hoping to find a door.

There was a big plate-glass door. It was locked. I went to grab my Hatzalah radio and break the window but couldn't find it. I grabbed the radio that I found in the street, which happened to be a Hatzalah radio that someone else lost, and started to bang on the glass, hoping to break it. It wouldn't break. Thank God I had that radio, because it was approximately twice the size of my regular radio. I don't know if anybody would have heard me banging on the glass with my regular radio. Somebody came to the door from inside and motioned to me to stop banging. He opened the door and let us in.

The lobby of this building was a little better than outside. There was light and water. We were all choking on the debris and smoke. We stayed in this lobby approximately fifteen minutes or so, till the second tower collapsed. Thank God I had picked up the radio, and I was able to communicate to let the other Hatzalah members know which building I was in and that I was alive.

It was horrendous listening to fellow Hatzalah members yelling for help on the radio not knowing exactly where they were or if they would survive. One member was yelling and crying that he was trapped and surrounded by fire all around and he didn't know where he was. Thinking back, this was a period of time, just listening to the Hatzalah radio, that we knew that we were being judged up Above.

At that point we were told to get out of the building for fear that it might also collapse. Someone handed out dust masks he had found. I grabbed a shirt and wet it and ripped it in half. I gave one half to a fireman so that we would have something to try to filter our breathing. As we ran out into the street back into this chaos, we didn't know what would fall on us.

I saw a Hatzalah ambulance. I jumped into it. There were other members in it already. We all needed oxygen badly. We were covered from head to toe in the debris. The ambulance was covered inside and outside with all this matter. The ambulance I was in was the one I came with to the city. I had my paramedic equipment in it, and it was also covered with this stuff. (I have no idea where my equipment is now — approximately $30,000 worth.) We all put on oxygen masks. We had to share it since we all needed it and there was only so much. We took turns. Each wanted the other one to have it, each saying, "You need it more than I." "*Mi k'amcha Yisrael* — Who is like Your nation, Israel!" I put a pulse oximeter on myself to see how much oxygen I was getting. It read 93 to 94 percent — a little low. Normal is 97 to 100 percent.

The ambulance wasn't able to go any further. We were at the waterfront a block or two from the towers. The police brought in boats to ferry people off Manhattan to Liberty Park in New Jersey. I knew I had to get out of there; I was having a hard time breathing.

I got off the ambulance and went toward the boats. They

were allowing women and children on first. I went to the front of the line and told them I was a paramedic, and they let me on the boat. I felt helpless standing there without any equipment trying to help people. There was a fireman who couldn't see because of the debris in his eyes. I found a bottle of water on the boat and tried flushing out his eyes. There was a woman from the chief medical examiner's office on the boat with a broken leg. The chief medical examiner had some lacerations on his hand. I told him I was glad I could meet him standing up! There was a person having an asthma attack. I tried my best to help the ones I was able to.

When we got to Liberty Park, there was a huge tent set up to triage patients coming off the boats. I helped some firemen. There was Fire Chief Murphy, who was having chest pains. I gave him some oxygen and got an ambulance crew to get him to a hospital. He was very thankful to myself and Hatzalah. I helped with some other patients for about an hour, when it all started to catch up with me.

I hadn't eaten all day. I had been in shul in the morning when I answered the Hatzalah call. From the call, I took my sons to yeshivah and then went straight to the city. On the way into the city I reminded myself to say Shema. I said the rest of the prayers at about one or two in the afternoon, while I was being treated for exhaustion and smoke inhalation. They took me to Bayonne Hospital, where the staff was unbelievable. They couldn't believe that we had survived. One Jewish doctor walked into the room. He looked at me and said, "*Baruch Hashem!*"

My roommate in the hospital was a paramedic from Metro

Care, who was in their command center when it got hit from debris from the building as it collapsed. He doesn't know how he got out of it. After all the dust settled, that command center was on its side in flames. He was banged up and will be okay, with God's help.

At the hospital I was quickly assessed in the emergency room and then sent up to a room where they did blood tests and a chest X-ray. Thank God, all looked okay. I was discharged at about four o'clock. Some Hatzalah members made their way to the hospital, and we were more than happy to see each other alive. Two of these guys were on the way into the building when it collapsed.

We had to get back to Brooklyn, but all the bridges and tunnels were closed. We went up to the cops and told them we were paramedics who were heading back to the city. They asked for some ID and let us through all the way to Brooklyn.

The miracles that we all experienced as individuals and as a group of Hatzalah members are indescribable. The *chessed* we all saw from Hashem is boundless. Thank God, all the Hatzalah members are accounted for, some with broken limbs and scratches and bruises – but alive!

We should all say *tehillim* and pray for those injured and those who are still trapped and unaccounted for.

There are numerous stories of miracles and *chessed* that we were privileged to witness and be a part of in this unfortunate situation.

When I got up this morning and said *Modeh Ani*, it had a whole different meaning. Prayer took a lot longer than usual. I wasn't in a rush to leave shul this morning. Life is too short and precious. Unfortunately, it sometimes takes a situation like this to wake us up.

May we all be inscribed in the Book of Life, and may we know of no more tragedies and witness the coming of Mashiach in our days.

# A HARROWING RESCUE

*By Yisrael Korn, as told to Sorah Shapiro*

*I am an accountant for McCann Erickson, an advertising agency. I had gotten to my office on West Fourteenth Street at 8:15 that day; I had gone to daven and say Selichos with an early minyan. Since I always keep my Hatzalah radio with me, I heard a call from home base that a plane had crashed and help was needed. The dispatcher asked the unit that called in the initial crash if it was a commuter plane, and he said it was a commercial airliner.*

I grabbed my radio and called a friend. I told him to go over there. I ran downstairs and over to St. Vincent's Hospital, which was around the corner, and I presented my Hatzalah identification as an EMT. They took me down to Ground Zero in their own ambulance, and I met up with three or four other Hatzalah ambulances in front of Tower One.

"An awesome sight" are the only words I can use to describe what I saw. There was a humongous hole, the biggest I had ever seen in my life, with flames and smoke coming out nonstop. Glass was falling. When we looked toward the ground, we saw so many people who had been injured that we didn't know where to begin. We started working on as many patients as we could. Eighteen minutes later we heard a noise. We looked up, and there was another airplane. At first we thought it was an accident.

I asked a police officer, "Is that a plane coming to help us?"

He said, "Look where it is going! We'd better get out of here fast!"

I put my arms under the patient I was working with and started dragging him, running backward.

When the plane hit, we saw a huge fireball. We were all thrown from the heat. It was so hot. We had many, many patients to work on. We ran back and forth between the hospitals. Things kept falling from the buildings. At one point I looked up and saw something that looked like a chair falling. As it got closer, I saw it was a person. The cops kept yelling to us, "Don't look up! Keep working on the patients!" It was raining people for about a half-hour. They kept jumping. They were either holding hands or by themselves.

When I and two other guys in a Hatzalah ambulance came back from St. Vincent's Hospital for the third time, we were about a block from Tower Two, which came down first. Another unit of Hatzalah had seven patients, whom they lined up against the building, some in trauma or shock. As soon as we put the first one into the back of the ambulance and I was inside, we heard a strange noise. It was a huge rumble, but it was five hundred times louder than the plane that had hit half an hour before. People starting screaming.

I had no idea what was going on. I was working on a patient in the back, and all of a sudden these other two Hatzalah guys jumped into the back of the ambulance. Two other people from the street jumped on. I thought it was another plane. We had been hearing stories all morning that ten other planes had been hijacked. We were just helping as many people as we could. None of us really knew what was going on.

Within about sixty to ninety seconds of that rumble, our ambulance was entirely covered with debris from top to bottom. We were buried alive. We heard screams over the Hatzalah radio. Members were saying Shema or crying, "Call my wife!" "Come and get me!"

There were no Hatzalah guys in the towers (because the dispatcher had ordered everyone to evacuate), but there were guys a block or a block and a half away. They were covered in smoke. When the towers came down, no one knew where they were. There was only darkness, and Hatzalah guys were screaming for help. Meanwhile, our ambulance was filling with smoke and dust. When the dispatcher asked us where we were, we said we didn't know; we needed help ourselves.

About twenty-five minutes later the scene became really harrowing. No one had come to help us. There were still people screaming on the radio for help. It was becoming difficult to breathe. Someone suggested that if we were indeed going to die, if this was it, if this was how our life would end, we should try to leave the world with a clean slate. We *klapped* "*Al Cheit*." We couldn't make any cell phone calls, because the cell phones were not working. I scribbled a little note to my wife.

Just as we thought that death was overtaking us, we heard the sound of rummaging through the rubble. All of a sudden we saw four firemen crawling through. One stuck his head through the window, which had broken when the building came down. He asked how many we were in there and if we were all okay. When we asked him how he knew we were there, he just shrugged and said he thought he had come upon a fire truck — he was searching for firemen. We were taken out and brought to New York University Hospital, where we were checked out and discharged.

## A LETTER FROM A HATZALAH MEMBER

*Sitting in my Yeshiva University dormitory room at nine in the morning, getting ready to take a shower, a loud announcement came screaming over my Hatzalah radio.*

"Attention all units! We need ambulances from all neighborhoods to start proceeding to lower Manhattan! We have reports that an airplane has just hit the World Trade Center!"

I flew down the stairs and ran outside to go to the Yeshiva University ambulance. I and three other members jumped into the ambulance, or bus, as it is called, and we went speeding down the West Side Highway with our lights and sirens. Another shocking report came over our radio: "We have reports that a second plane has just hit the Twin Towers!" At this point we knew what we were going to be facing. Or so we thought.

As we got closer to lower Manhattan, we could see the towers burning at the top but still standing tall in the sky. It was time to work. We drove our bus to John Street, where we began looking for patients. We were at no loss for people to help. Doctors, EMTs, paramedics, firemen, nurses, and anyone with any minute medical training hustled and bustled back and forth, trying to find the most serious patients and get them to the hospital.

We had only managed to get a few critical patients loaded and to the hospital when the worst part began. "Code one! Code one! The scene is not safe! All units evacuate the area immediately! Tower One is coming down!"

But it was too late. The ground under us began to rumble. I almost got knocked off my feet. It sounded like a subway car was about to ride right over our heads, which would have been a better option than what was about to occur. Everyone began to run in every direction, but there was nowhere to run.

I froze. I didn't know where to go or what to do. I looked up at the sky, and there it was, coming straight at me. A massive storm of black soot and ash came hailing down on us at such speed that it hurled people and cars out of its way. Tower One had come down in a mean way. I ran and, *baruch Hashem*, I was able to dive into a tiny shoe store just as the door was being slammed shut. I and about twenty other crying victims were to be left to die in a shoe store in lower Manhattan.

When the small store began to fill with black soot and smoke, we all rushed up the stairs to the even smaller attic. But it was of no use. The smoke joined us up the stairs, and it was getting hard to breathe. There was just no air. I frantically called for help on the radio and begged someone to come get us out.

"H-Base, I am trapped inside a store at 1 John Street with twenty patients, one of whom is an asthmatic. Smoke is filling the room, and we can't breathe."

I called for help, but I knew it wouldn't come. Everyone was trapped from the collapse of the tower, and we were just another group of helpless victims.

I would love to tell a story about how I said Shema and jumped for joy to die *al kiddush Hashem*, but that's not how it went. I was scared. Really scared! I think I may have gotten in half a "*Shir HaMa'alos*," but I couldn't finish it. There was just too much going through my head. I did not want to die.

Then a miracle happened. Okay, maybe it was just a big firefighter, but I'll call him a miracle. He was able to get the door open and told us all to hold our breaths and run north as fast as we could. Let me tell you, north, south, east, west, I have no clue. I just ran. With no visibility and no air to breathe, I ran into the back streets. It was totally Heaven-sent that just as I couldn't hold my breath any longer I ran right into the back of an ambulance.

I banged on the door, and they let me in to get my first breath of fresh air. After a little oxygen and a few seconds of rest, I came back to reality. I didn't believe it at first, but I began to realize that I wasn't going to die. Riding with us was a doctor from Brooklyn, six Hatzalah members, and five patients. We transported them all to NYU Medical Center, and from there we restocked and went back to help more people.

NYU Hospital was medically ready for thousands of patients, but they didn't come. Few people were found at this point. We remained until midnight, treating a few firefighters and other rescue workers but almost no people from the buildings. It was a sad day for all of us.

The next day I took the train back downtown and hopped

a ride with a police car to Ground Zero. It was not to be believed! Most of the day I stood a few feet from the tower, which was now on the West Side Highway, digging through rubble to find bodies and maybe even trapped people. Standing on top of these innocent people made me cringe. My friend and I dug up shoes, business cards, fans, clothes, you name it. It was all there, scattered at our feet. We treated some rescue workers throughout the day until we were evacuated by a police boat for fear that more buildings were going to fall.

So what should be taken from all this? Well, I don't know, and at three in the morning I don't have many insightful thoughts. I can tell you, though, that I'm changed from it. I thought my life was over, and that's a hard feeling to forget. But looking back I know one thing. The Creator was behind this from start to finish. We don't know why, and we can't even try to explain it. This was the most terrible thing I have ever seen.

We must strengthen ourselves in this terrible time of pain and suffering and use our sorrows to enable us to really concentrate when we daven this Rosh HaShanah and Yom Kippur. I think that the davening should have new meaning to all of us, and our *kavanah* should be that much greater. I hope that through our *tefillah, teshuvah,* and *tzedakah* we will overcome this terrible decree and will merit to see the coming of Mashiach speedily in our days.

# CHAPTER SEVEN

# Adding It Up

The date of the attack was 9/11 (9+1+1 = 11).

911 is the phone number for help.

September 11 is the 254th day of the year (2+5+4 = 11).

After September 11 there are 111 days left until the end of the year.

119 is the beginning of the telephone area code to Iraq and Iran (1+1+9 = 11).

The Twin Towers, standing side by side, look like the number 11.

The state of New York was the 11th state added to the Union.

Independence Day is July 4 (7+4 = 11).

"New York City" has 11 letters.

"Afghanistan" has 11 letters.

"The Pentagon" has 11 letters.

"Shanksville," in Pennsylvania, the crash site of the fourth plane has 11 letters.

"Air Force One" has 11 letters.

"George W. Bush" has 11 letters.

The name Ramzi Yousef (convicted of orchestrating the attack on the WTC in 1993) has 11 letters.

The first plane to hit the towers was American Airlines Flight 11. It departed Boston Airport at 7:59 A.M. and crashed at 8:46 A.M. after flying for 47 minutes (4+7 = 11).

Flight 11 had 92 passengers on board, 11 of whom were crew members (9+2 = 11).

American Airlines Flight 77, which crashed into the Pentagon, departed Dulles Airport bound for Los Angeles at 8:10 A.M. and crashed at 9:44 after flying for 92 minutes (9+2 = 11). It had 65 passengers on board (6+5 = 11).

United Airlines Flight 175, which crashed into the south tower of the World Trade Center, had 65 passengers on board, not counting crew (6+5 =11).

United Airlines Flight 93 crashed southeast of Pittsburgh with 38 passengers (3+8 = 11).

Quite a coincidence, no? Is it of any significance? You decide.

# CHAPTER EIGHT

# Torah Perspectives

## (IN ALPHABETICAL ORDER)

### RABBI YAAKOV BENDER

*ROSH YESHIVAH, DARCHEI TORAH AND MESIVTA CHAIM SHLOMO,*
*FAR ROCKAWAY, NEW YORK*
*Based on an address at Kinus Teshuvah (September 15, 2001)*

Two *pesukim* in *parashas Vayeilech* describe the state of the world in the days when it will be beset with trouble: *klal Yisrael* will stop doing mitzvos and will do *aveiros*. HaKadosh Baruch Hu tells Moshe Rabbeinu that in those terrible days, when *klal Yisrael* will have fallen into the depths of degradation, "I am going to hide My face." It will be a time of *hester panim*, as Chazal call it. HaKadosh Baruch Hu says, "I will be nowhere to be found, because of all the terrible *aveiros* you have done."

This is a terrible, terrible curse, say Chazal, His not being there — having no one to turn to. In the worst of times, knowing that He is up there is reassuring, but when He goes into hiding, that's a bitter curse.

It occurred to me that concealed within that curse may be a blessing.

There are two types of hiding. There is the obvious kind. In World War II, when people went into hiding, they didn't want the Nazis to know their whereabouts. They didn't even tell their closest family where they were. The other type is less obvious. For example, a child is playing hide-and-seek with his father, and the father keeps saying, "I can't find you. I can't find you." Suddenly the child bursts out with "*Tatte*, you can't find me?" Then, of course, the father does find him. What is the difference between these two types of hiding, the one where one doesn't want to be found and the one where one does?

I think it is simple. If a person declares, "I am going into hiding," it indicates that he wants to be found. But if he doesn't say anything – he just disappears, he's gone, no one knows where he is – that means he doesn't want to be found. When the Torah tells us that HaKadosh Baruch Hu proclaims that He's going into hiding, that means He's inviting us to look for Him. "If you look for Me, you will find Me," He says.

What would Rav Elazar Menachem Mann Shach, *zt"l*, have said about today's state of affairs? He says it clearly in the introduction to his monumental work, *Avi Ezri*. The verses say that HaKadosh Baruch Hu said, "I will become very angry on that day, and I will desert *klal Yisrael*, and I will go into hiding. They will become prey to the nations of the world. Many terrible things will befall them. And the nation will say on that day, 'Because we did not perceive HaKadosh Baruch Hu's Presence among us. We did not care about Him.' Because of these utterances all the terrible things will befall you.' " Rav Shach says, "In the beginning of the *pasuk* it says, '*Ra'os rabbos v'tzaros* – Many terrible things and troubles will find you.' At the end it says only *ra'os* will find you. What happened to the *tzaros*?"

Rav Shach explains that there's a major difference between *ra'os* and *tzaros*. What happened on Tuesday (September 11) and what's been happening in Eretz Yisrael for the last eleven months, that's *ra'os*. That's terrible. You can't deny the *ra'os*; they're obvious. *Tzaros*, on the other hand, are in the mind. When a person feels *tza'ar*, pain, he doesn't know where to go or where to move. It's all in the mind. But when he discovers that there is a *Ribbono shel olam* in the world — even though He's in hiding — he will no longer feel the *tzaros*.

The *ra'os* cannot be denied. There will be so many *ra'os*, you won't know what to do with yourself. But if you realize that the *Ribbono shel olam* is in your midst, that He is there, that He is close to you, you will have the *ra'os*, but you won't have the *tzaros* of the mind.

The hiding is only temporary. The *tzaros rabbos* are not there — only the *ra'os rabbos*, which will quickly disappear with the coming of Mashiach speedily in our days.

## RABBI SHMUEL BERENBAUM

*ROSH YESHIVAH, MIRRER YESHIVA, BROOKLYN, NEW YORK*
*From a shmuess to yeshivah alumni, adapted by Moshe Schapiro*
*(Yated Ne'eman, November 2, 2001)*
*Reprinted with permission*

The real purpose of affliction in this world is not to punish man for his sins but rather to compel him to take stock of his deeds and to repent for his sins. This is how we should view the cataclysmic events that have swept through the United States in recent weeks.

Of course, this is easier said than done. When a person is

numbed by the chilling aftershock of personal tragedy, he is in
no state to focus on the ultimate meaning of life. To do so
would require him to rise above a human being's natural limitations. Yet this is precisely what is expected of a Jew.

We learn this concept from the *pasuk* "Today all of you are
standing before Hashem your God – your leaders, the heads
of your tribes, your elders, your law enforcers, all the men of
Israel" (*Devarim* 29:9).

In reference to this verse Rashi writes, "Why is *parashas
Nitzavim* juxtaposed to the curses [mentioned in the previous
parashah]? Because when the Jewish people heard the ninety-
eight curses...their faces turned yellow. 'Who can withstand
those [curses]?' they said. At this point Moshe began to pacify
them: 'Today all of you are standing before Hashem your God.
You angered Hashem many times,' [Moshe said to them,] 'yet
He did not destroy you, and here you are, standing before
Him.' "

The Kli Yakar points out that at first glance Moshe's reaction is difficult to understand. After all, what was he trying to
do, soften the Torah's message, *chas v'shalom*? The Torah
warned the Jewish people that if they would sin, they would be
punished. Moshe, in his efforts to soothe the people, appeared
to be trying to minimize this reward-and-punishment formula.

Perhaps the solution to the Kli Yakar's question is that the
Jewish people's faces did not "turn yellow" from the shocking
news that such curses would befall them when they sinned –
they were familiar with this formula by now. Rather, their
faces "turned yellow" from the realization that they would be

expected to react to affliction by taking stock of their deeds and repenting for their sins. How could they live up to such high expectations? they wondered. To endure punishment submissively is one thing. To rise above the pain and actively repent for one's sins is another thing entirely.

In this context, Moshe Rabbeinu's dialogue with the people is easier to understand. "You committed many sins during our sojourn in the desert and endured great punishment as a result," Moshe in essence said to them. "Yet in every instance you managed to rise above the pain and internalize the message that you must do *teshuvah*. This ability of yours to repent during times of affliction is the reason you are still alive today. Do not think you are not up to the task. You have done it before, and you will do it again. In this sense, affliction has strengthened you."

This interpretation clarifies Moshe Rabbeinu's intent. He did not try to dilute the Torah's message; rather, he tried to instill in the people the confidence and conviction they needed to rise to the challenge and use the pain of affliction as a catalyst for *teshuvah*. More importantly, he tried to give them hope. Moshe knew that when a person is in a state of depression he becomes emotionally paralyzed and cannot accomplish anything. "You are here," Moshe told them, "standing tall, and you have the ability to withstand and do everything that is required."

## What Is Expected of Us?

This is how we should relate to the September 11 attacks and to the terrorist actions that are still unfolding today. They are signals from *Shamayim* that the time has come for all of us to do *teshuvah*, to learn from our mistakes. Getting depressed is not the Jewish response to such situations. We have to show resilience, just as our ancestors did in the desert, and rise to the occasion.

No one is saying that it is easy to overcome the rising sense of panic and depression sweeping through the country and to focus on the deeper meaning of things. Unfortunately, Moshe Rabbeinu is not here to infuse us with courage. He cannot be here with us to help us face this challenge and dispel the mood of depression that is settling into the society around us. But that doesn't change the fact that this is the task at hand.

It's time for us to sit up and take notice. To learn from our mistakes. Hashem is telling us something.

How else can one understand the events that took place? Consider the facts: a single individual, without the aid of tanks, warplanes, or cruise missiles, manages to strike at the symbols of America's military and economic might – the Pentagon and the World Trade Center. He and a band of wild-eyed followers throw the most powerful nation on earth into a state of panic and an economic recession. World markets grind to a halt. Both houses of Congress are closed down. The Supreme Court building is evacuated. A nation goes to war. All because of a fanatic hiding in a cave somewhere.

And why did this have to happen to America, of all countries? In two thousand years of *galus* Jews have never had as much freedom and safety as they enjoy today in the United States. The American people have helped the Jews in Eretz Yisrael as no other nation on earth. If the attacks had to happen, why couldn't the victims have been nations that have a long history of anti-Semitic atrocities, such as Germany, Poland, or Spain? Why did it have to be the United States? Obviously Hashem is trying to tell us something. To shock us into a state of mental alertness. To wake us from our slumber. To tell us that the time has come to do a little spiritual reckoning and fix the things that have gone wrong.

The murderers who have brought about the deaths of so many innocent people are merely *shelichim*. As long as we put off the task at hand — to do *teshuvah* — they will continue to sow death and destruction. But the moment we fulfill our mission, they will be destroyed.

## Why the Jews Are Always to Blame

Shortly before Moshe's death, Hashem said to him: "When you go and lie with your ancestors, this nation shall rise up and stray after the alien gods of the land into which they are coming. They will thus abandon Me and violate the covenant that I have made with them" (*Devarim* 31:16).

In the very next *pasuk*, Hashem adds: "I will then display anger against them and abandon them. I will hide My face from them, and they will be [their enemies'] prey. Beset by many evils and troubles, they will say, 'It is because my God is no longer with me that these evils have befallen us.' On that day I will utterly hide My face because of all the evils they have done in turning to alien gods" (*Devarim* 31:17–18).

The Ramban asks an obvious question: Why will Hashem "hide His face" when the Jewish people will finally come to the realization that the tragedies they endure are a result of their estrangement from Hashem? Surely their recognition of the reward-and-punishment correlation will be a step in the right direction. Why, then, will Hashem respond by "utterly hiding His face"?

The *pesukim* refer to two different sins. *Pasuk* 16 refers to the sin of "violating the covenant" with Hashem by worshiping idols, other deities, money, power, or any other false gods. The Jewish people's estrangement from Hashem in turn causes Him to remove His divine protection from them, thus exposing them to the nations of the world, who overpower them.

The following verse refers to a second and perhaps more serious sin: that of recognizing Hashem but failing to internalize the lessons one can glean from affliction and delaying in doing *teshuvah* and rectifying faults. At this point Hashem "utterly hides His face" from the Jewish people.

This sequence of events is not a form of active punishment but one that comes naturally. The Jews turn their backs on Hashem. He abandons them. Lacking His protection, they become prey for their enemies. They realize the root of the problem yet fail to do *teshuvah*. And then Hashem conceals Himself from them even more.

Unfortunately, we see the fulfillment of this *pasuk* almost daily. All you have to do is read the newspaper headlines.

When Jews are slaughtered by Palestinian terrorists, the world hardly says a word. But when an Arab terrorist on his way to commit an attack against helpless civilians is killed by security forces, a great hue and cry erupts throughout the world. Front-page headlines decry the brutal killing of yet another "Palestinian civilian." No mention is made of the fact that this particular "civilian" was heavily armed and was on his way to slaughter innocent Jewish women and children.

We are still surprised when this happens, but really we shouldn't be. This is the natural state of the world – the Jews are prey to the nations of the world. Things work differently only when Hashem protects us. At such times, the world turns its attention to other matters and allows us to live in peace. But when we turn away from Him, He abandons us and lets us fend for ourselves, which, of course, we cannot. And then the world comes after us.

By this token, we should be very thankful that we were not held responsible for the attacks against America. According to the natural laws of the world, our enemies should have tried to blame it on us. Hashem intervened on our behalf in this instance and silenced the voices of those who indeed tried to ascribe the attacks to Israel's policies toward the Arabs.

Therefore, the next time you read a biased report against Eretz Yisrael, or hear a diplomat utter unfair criticism against that country, remember that it has nothing to do with poor media coverage or ineffectual public relations tactics. It is simply the natural consequence of Hashem's having removed His protection from us.

## America and the Jews

Before September 11, we thought living in America was different. Yes, of course we knew we were in *galus*. But it was a pleasant sort of *galus*. It was the kind you hardly felt, and everyone felt secure. Jews and non-Jews alike would go to work without fear of impending doom. The thought that we might not return home never crossed our minds. In that innocent age, the worst thing we could imagine happening was being mugged.

But those days are over.

And the Torah tells us why: "They will thus abandon Me and violate the covenant that I have made with them" (*Devarim* 31:16). Note that the *pasuk* does not say that the Jews sinned, only that they abandoned Hashem. In other words, they placed their faith in other entities and relied on them for protection instead of relying on Hashem.

We placed our faith in America and everything it stands for: financial stability – the World Trade Center; military might – the Pentagon; freedom – to get on a plane and go wherever you want without having your bags checked and your body frisked.

In a single sharp blow, Hashem showed the world just how durable America really is. "If you think that you don't require My protection any longer," He said to us, "if you think you have found a new home in America, then I will leave you to your own devices. Good luck!"

Then America collapsed.

The same thing happened in Eretz Yisrael. After the Six-Day War, bumper stickers everywhere declared, "Trust in the Israel Defense Forces," a play on words on the more traditional statement "Trust in Hashem."

Where is the vaunted IDF today? Jews are being bombed and shot daily in the streets of Israel's main cities, and the army cannot do anything to stop it.

We, however, can do something about it. If we would acknowledge that we need Hashem's protection, that nothing can replace it, and that we cannot exist without it, then Hashem will assume responsibility for our protection once again. This is how we could make the nightmare stop. Right now.

It's a matter of showing that we care that Hashem's protection is important to us.

Shortly before World War II, the Polish authorities passed a law prohibiting *shechitah*. "Why are 3 million Jews prevented from eating meat?" asked Rav Yerucham Levovitz of Mir. "The reason is that Hashem sees that we do not fulfill the mitzvos with *simchah*. He sees that we complain that it's difficult to keep the mitzvos and that we do it almost as though we were doing Him a favor. And so, perceiving that we do not value the opportunity to perform the mitzvos, He takes them away from us, one by one."

The same concept can be applied to our generation. Since we do not value Hashem's protection, He takes it away from us.

## Kiddush Hashem

Another way to understand why this terrible tragedy took place is to consider the impact that we, as Jews, have had on society. The role of a Jew is to sanctify Hashem's Name in the eyes of the nations, as the *pasuk* says, "All the nations of the world will realize that Hashem's Name is upon you, and they will be in awe of you" (*Devarim* 28:10). And in *Yeshayah* it says, "Everyone is called by my Name, for I have created him for my glory, I have formed him, I have made him" (*Yeshayahu* 43:7).

But how well have we fared in this respect? How often do the non-Jews among us look at us and think to themselves, *So there is a God in the world after all?*

They take it easy, and we take it easy. They get involved in the material world, and we get involved in the material world. They buy full-length mink coats, and we buy full-length mink coats. They put their dishes in the dishwasher, and we put our dishes in the dishwasher. They buy take-out food, and we buy take-out food. All of us are after the same easy lifestyle, with perhaps one or two minor modifications.

We run to shul, daven quickly so as to get to work on time, occasionally engage in questionable business practices, run back home ten minutes before Shabbos, fall asleep at the Shabbos table on Friday night, sit back and relax on Sunday, and then it's back to work on Monday.

How much enthusiasm do we show for the mitzvos? What is more important in our eyes – *tefillah* and Torah study or making money? Which subject do our children hear us talking about most often?

If we would have gone through our daily routine with an eye to observing halachah scrupulously, perhaps it would not have taken such a horrendous disaster to communicate to American society the concept that there is a God in the world. Perhaps if people would have seen more Jews running their businesses according to the halachic definition of honesty in monetary matters, they would have come to this conclusion before.

There are many ways to proclaim God's existence to the world. Killing thousands of people in a brutal fashion and destroying one of the most famous symbols of civilization is one way. Refusing to speak *lashon hara* about someone when the opportunity arises is another.

Our influence on the world around us cannot be underestimated.... Perhaps if we would have demonstrated more often what it means to be sensitive to the pain of others and given more *tzedakah*, it would not have been necessary for Americans to set up emergency relief funds for the victims of the attacks. They could have learned the same lesson from our actions instead of having to learn it on their own from their own flesh and blood. Perhaps if we would have shared in the *simchah* of our fellow Jews instead of feeling jealousy, it would not have been necessary for Americans to cheer the latest bombing raid on Kabul. They could have learned how to cheer the success of one's fellow man from us.

Rav Yisrael Salanter used to say that if we would keep Shabbos in strict accordance with halachah, we would have a positive influence on non-Jewish society. If we would behave as the Torah prescribes, the world would look totally different. It all depends on us. Through our actions, we have the power to determine whether good or evil will reign.

## The Power of the Individual

The Chafetz Chaim would say that when he was a youth he tried to rectify the entire world, but it didn't work. Then he tried to at least rectify Lithuania, but, alas, that also did not happen. He decided to try to change the city of Radin, but in this, too, he failed. In the end he tried to change himself, and here he finally succeeded.

As a result of the Chafetz Chaim's spiritual development,

Radin gradually changed for the better. The sphere of righteousness rippled outward, and eventually it spread throughout Lithuania. In time, the Chafetz Chaim's message reached Jews throughout the world. Rav Elchanan Wasserman said that as a result of his efforts the world did become a better place.

In reference to the impact of *teshuvah* on a person, the Rambam writes, "How great is the merit of *teshuvah*! Yesterday [the sinner] was separated from Hashem, the God of Israel...yet today, after repenting, he merits to adhere to the Shechinah.... He davens and is answered immediately.... And he performs mitzvos, and they are gratefully and joyously accepted [by Hashem]..." (*Hilchos Teshuvah* 7:7).

From here we see the power of *teshuvah* — even in a cave where *teshuvah* does not immediately eliminate every last trace of sin, nevertheless, it enables the sinner to adhere to the Shechinah by removing the partitions created by the *cheit* which separates him from Hashem.

The Chafetz Chaim proved that every Jew has the power to change the world.

## RABBI AVROHOM BLUMENKRANTZ

*RAV OF BAIS MEDRASH ATERES YISRAEL, FAR ROCKAWAY, NEW YORK*
*Excerpted from an address given before Yom Kippur 5762*

We are in the *ikvesa d'Meshicha*. Chazal explain to us that in the last *galus*, the *galus Edom*, prior to Mashiach's coming, we are going to have to go through a *galus Yishmael*. Never in the history of mankind has the world been in a *galus Yishmael*. Yishmael has taken over the world. The world is afraid of Yishmael. He has the oil and the money, and he has the aspect of *pere adam*.

We are in the *ikvesa d'Meshicha*. It's just a question of how much longer. We are in the midst of the War of Gog U'Magog. It started a while ago with World War I and World War II. Whatever was prophesied that would happen to *klal Yisrael*, the terrible *tzaros* that *klal Yisrael* would experience in the War of Gog U'Magog, has happened. What is left are the skirmishes and little wars that still make up the War of Gog U'Magog. Hopefully they will end soon, with the coming of Mashiach ben David.

In such a time, one of the most important things we Jews have to realize is that the *Ribbono shel olam* wants all of His children. *Klal Yisrael* today is made up of close to 15 million people, but so many of them are so far away from Hashem. Before He brings Mashiach, He wants his children — all of them — back. People and organizations have seen unusual success in bringing back lost Jews. There is something for us to do also.

In this time of *ikvesa d'Meshicha*, we all go about doing our own thing. This shows in the way we talk, the way we express ourselves: "I'll see you tomorrow." "I'm going to do this." "It's my accomplishment." We don't recognize that Hashem is behind all our actions. So what happens? Suddenly comes a September 11, and two planes crash into the most powerful, mighty nation of the world, into the symbol of economy and strength in the world, and within minutes those buildings collapse and become dust, and we begin thinking about the lives of people being taken away in such horrible ways. At the same time, we hear the stories about how people were spared through the workings of *yad Hashem*, and we suddenly begin to realize that the Creator is here. But that's not what He really wants.

He wants our Shabbos and *yom tov* to help us. He wants us to go on in our day-to-day life and recognize His Presence. And it is that recognition that is so important, because if I recognize that He is right in front of me, that He is above me, that He is at my right side and at my left, it's going to have an influence on me, and therefore I will act and behave differently. Do you know what the Creator wants of *klal Yisrael*? He wants its best, its potential. He wants *klal Yisrael* to be a kingdom of priests and a holy nation. Anything less than that and we are not living up to what He expects of us; we are not living up to our potential.

This episode, this phenomenon we experienced on September 11, what does it leave us with? We said *tehillim*. We gathered in the thousands. We cried. After all that, they tell us to go back to normal. With our many sins, it is obvious how it relates to *klal Yisrael*, and we cannot afford it. This has to leave an impression on us. If we are going to let it pass and let it become just a part of history, we will have failed to meet the objective of the Creator, especially now.

In the month this has happened, Elul, the fish tremble. They are scared. Angels tremble. Can you imagine? If they tremble and fear, what should we do? There is a judgment: Who shall live and who shall perish? How many will leave this world and how many will be born?

There are so many people who are living in a vegetable state. Look what happened to those buildings! The Creator comes in

— if the shofar didn't do it and nothing else accomplished it — and brings on such a catastrophe.

We must wake up. We must look at the *yad Hashem* in a way that can influence us. It is possible to do mitzvos and yet not to be influenced positively by them, and this is what is happening to us. We daven every day, learn every day, do mitzvos every day, and keep Shabbos, and yet it's not having an impact on us.

This is what the Creator reminded us. We are required to do mitzvos. Before Pesach you *krechtz* ten thousand times, but with all the *krechtz*ing you didn't accomplish your objective. You did the mitzvah, no question about it. But did it influence you? No. Shabbos comes, and we don't put effort into it. We don't get the point. The sweat a person secretes when preparing for Shabbos becomes the soap that washes away his sins. How can we lose such an opportunity?

Shabbos by the *tisch*, everything is so beautiful. How do we spend the Shabbos? Is the radiance of Shabbos there? Do we sit at the Shabbos table with *simchah v'tuv leivav*? The man who all week is falling off his feet from exhaustion and sits down to the Shabbos table with radiance and *simchah* and says to his children, "Children, it's *Shabbos kodesh*! Let's sing *zemiros*!" — this man has earned *techiyas hameisim*.

How many people feel uncomfortable about having *sefarim* in the dining room? They think it's not very nice. But we are the people of the book! There should be a *sefer* in every room.

Rabbi Gifter, *zt"l*, once came back from seeing a *frum* eye doctor in Philadelphia, elated by what he saw in his house.

"Wherever I went, in every room, in his home and his office, there were *sefarim*." If we are proud of it — these are little things, but it is those little things that bring out the feeling of the Presence of Hashem — then we are proud to be Yidden. The desire to have the Shechinah in our home, to make sure we don't miss the opportunity, to make sure that there is an atmosphere of pleasantness in our home, for no other reason but to keep the Presence of the Shechinah there.

When the husband comes in from the street, which today is filled with immorality, greet him, not with "Hello," but with "Shalom, how was your day?" and then go back to whatever you were doing. You don't have to be dressed in a wedding gown. Just be a mensch. Imagine someone important is knocking on your door. Would you go to greet him in a housecoat that's torn and stained? You wouldn't. Don't do that to your husband.

A husband has to appreciate his wife. I don't envy a man who would undertake even five minutes of a woman's job — the responsibility of having children, nursing children, bringing up children, feeding the family. This is an unusually difficult job. The women deserve all the appreciation in the world. If there are any differences of opinion in the home, they have to be aired in a nice way. If they can't be resolved, that's what *rabbanim* are here for. We're at your service seven days a week, twenty-four hours a day. We have beepers, and we have cell phones. But you have to subordinate yourself to *da'as Torah*, and then you will feel the Shechinah.

We have to know that the Hashem whose Presence we must recognize is our Hashem, that he is the God of each of us, that He is watching over every single Jew. The pride of Hashem is that He took each of us by His hand and led us out of Mitzrayim. No one should think that Hashem is not going to bother with him, because it's not true.

How do you know when you've done enough *teshuvah*? When you reach the level of "*Shuvah Yisrael ad Hashem Elokecha*" — when you come to the realization that the Creator of the world is your God, that He is ruler over you, watching you. If you recognize that God rules over you, not just over other people, how can you do an *aveirah*?

If we show Him some effort on our part, that the mitzvos influence us to be better people, and we act the way He wants us to act, as a "*mamleches kohanim v'goy kadosh*," He will pour and pour his blessings over us until we say, "Enough!" And He will continue to pour and pour with great joy.

We have to resolve that our only desire is to do the will of Hashem.

## RABBI SHLOMO BREVDA

*TORAH AUTHOR AND LECTURER*
*From an address delivered after Sukkos 5762*
*on his return from Eretz Yisrael*

There is no doubt that we have entered the period called "*chevlo shel Mashiach*." Rashi with his prophetic vision explains "*chevlo shel Mashiach*" as the fears and sufferings that will prevail at that time due to the ravaging troops of the nations. Rashi goes out of his way to emphasize the "fears," that is, the panic. This is exactly what we are feeling today. All you need is for someone to get a letter with a little powder in it, and there's fear in two or three states, and you shut down post offices, hospitals. If you travel over a bridge now, wherever you go, there are police all over. We've never seen this before. We are in that period.

When did it begin? Last year when in Eretz Yisrael our enemies began to spill our blood on an almost daily basis. And it's quite possible that it began during the Second World War, when they spilled the blood of hundreds, thousands, millions of our people. People were gassed to death and their bodies cremated. Before they gassed them, they tortured and abused them as never seen before on the face of this earth. At the same time, the Jews of North Africa and the Middle East were uprooted from their homes, where, for many centuries, their ancestors had lived and thrived. This could have been the beginning of *chevlo shel Mashiach.*

It's possible that the First World War was the real beginning, because – as I was told by one of my rebbes – when the Chafetz Chaim was informed that the armistice agreement had been signed by all parties of the First World War and that there would be peace, he did not accept it. "Peace?" he said. "*Es vet noch gissen un gissen* – The blood will flow and flow." He knew that the First World War was just the beginning of the bloodshed. So maybe that was the beginning.

However, history chronicles the beginning of *chevlo shel Mashiach.* These are such trying times that one of the *chazal* in the Gemara issued this statement: "*Yeisei v'lo achminei...* – Let Mashiach arrive, but I would rather not be present in that generation." The Creator accepted his *tefillah.*

Poor us. We are here today to face it. Find me a Jewish

household without a major problem today. It's unbelievable. How many fine Jewish men cannot find *shidduchim*! How many fine Jewish ladies cannot find *shidduchim*! It is a nightmare to think of it! How many fine families are suffering from *tza'ar gidul banim*, with major spiritual problems with both boys and girls! How many tragedies, young men and young women dying, leaving households of eight or ten children! How much *machlokes* is going on today! This is the real *chevlo shel Mashiach*. We're in this period now.

It is not worthwhile for any of us to delve into what the Creator did here in America to try to gain a deep understanding of what He is aiming for, what the consequences will be, why it happened. It's a waste of time. No one can properly understand what the Creator is doing with His world today. However, we have a tremendous plus over the nations. We believe that the Creator is running everything. We know that, whatever happened on that day, He was fully in charge.

The person who actually believes in his own prowess is now a pitiful, bewildered individual, because he doesn't know how the attack occurred. He has complaints against the FBI, the CIA, Bush, and he relies on their assurances that from now on they're going to beef up security.

We, however, know that the Creator was in charge of everything. And I'm telling you, don't try to understand what and why He did what He did. You're not going to understand it. But at least know that He did it.

Why do I say you won't understand? There are times when the Creator performs an act in this world, and He reveals to the world that He is performing the act. Such an act bolsters *emunah* and *bitachon*. Such an act sometimes brings forth a *shirah b'ruach hakodesh*. Such an act is remembered forever. But there are times when He performs acts of *hester panim* — He conceals that He is doing it. At first glance you don't realize it is an act of the Creator. But if you look into it deeply, you will eventually see that it was the Hand of the Creator. That's *hester panim*. That was the *nes* of Purim — a concealed miracle.

About our times it says in the Torah, *"V'anochi haster astir panai bayom hahu* — I will hide My face on that day." That's a *hester* within a *hester*. There is no one who can fully understand what's going on. Hashem is hiding completely and camouflaging what He is doing here. That's why it is a waste of time for Jewish men to think into it — it is *bitul Torah*. And for women, it is spending time on nonsense. We are in *chevlo shel Mashiach*, and the Creator is preparing for the *geulah sheleimah*. Why He is doing it this way, what will be the immediate consequence and the long-term consequence, don't you dare think into it! You will be wasting your time. It's not Torah — you don't have to learn it.

I've been saying for the past year that no one understands anything today. Two weeks ago in Eretz Yisrael a very prominent young man asked me to come to speak in his yeshivah. He is very close (actually family) to one of today's *gedolei hador*. He said to me that this *adam gadol* told him that we are in a state of *"haster astir"* today, which means no one understands anything. Anyone who tells you he really understands all these matters is speaking falsely.

When I was speaking in one of the American girls' seminaries in Yerushalayim before Rosh HaShanah, one of the principals told me after my *drashah* that her in-laws have a *kehillah* in Boston. A young lady who davens there flies to Los Angeles on business a few times a month. She always arrives ten minutes before the flight and gets right on the plane. All the officials know her. On that day, she got to the airport ten minutes before the flight, but they told her at the gate, "Sorry, madam, the gate is closed!" She began to bawl them out. "How dare you! I always come at this time!" But they stood there, stone-faced. "The gate is closed, madam," they repeated. That saved her life. That plane crashed into the Twin Towers.

Another Orthodox Jewish lady who worked in the Twin Towers habitually came to work late. The day before the occurrence, her boss called her into his office and told her if she ever came late again, even one minute, she would be fired. She made every effort to be on time the next day, but she came two minutes late, which, to her, was early. As she walked in, the boss rushed toward her, pointed to the clock, and said, "I told you if you're even one minute late, you'll be fired, and you are! Get out!" She didn't know what hit her. She flew out of the office and down in the elevator upset. When the plane struck the building, he was killed and she was saved.

There are so many stories, all of which prove my point: the Creator was completely in charge. Whatever He wanted to do, He did. Whomever he wanted to save, He saved.

We must learn a very important lesson from this. The Vilna Gaon said in various places that when the Creator wants to bring a punishment on earth He has three very potent legions: fire, wind, and water. He could have done what He did to the Twin Towers and to the Pentagon through a minor earthquake or some other "natural" way. There are times when He appoints a *shaliach* to do the work, sometimes *resha'im*. Whom did He choose to do this piece of work? Of all the *resha'im* in the world, who got the job? *Bnei Yishmael* and their followers. This is a tremendous lesson for us.

Some time ago a Jewish Orthodox elementary school asked me to give a special lecture to the eighth grade on the topic of *derech eretz*. What was my theme? On the sixth day of Creation, in the morning, the animals were created. Half a day later, in the afternoon, man was created. Man was given a *neshamah*, the mental capacities of a human being, superior to animals. Obviously the Creator demands that every action of a human being should portray that he is not an animal, that he is a mensch. We should clearly see the difference between a mensch and an animal, and that difference is *derech eretz*.

What is the character and personality of an animal? An animal is an extremely self-centered, egoistic, selfish being that takes into account nothing besides its desire at the moment. Nothing surrounding this animal matters to it, only its desire. For example, an animal is standing at point A. Two or three hundred yards away is a weaker animal. The first animal is hungry. It decides to devour that other animal. What does it do? It rushes forward, all three hundred yards, corners the other animal, grabs it, tears off its limbs, and eats it. And Brevda is there, and he goes over to interview the animal.

"Animal, I understand you are hungry. But tell me, do you realize what you did on the way to capturing your prey? You uprooted twenty-five fruit trees and trampled on a whole vegetable garden. Why did you have to do it? It didn't gain you anything. You could have gone on a detour around the vineyard and around the vegetable garden, and then you would have captured your animal. You'd have the same food. Why did you have to cause so much destruction on the way, which no one benefited from?"

The animal looks at me and says, "I don't know what you're talking about. All that exists in this world is me and my lunch, that's all. What is this talk of fruit trees and vegetable gardens and destruction? It doesn't fit into my psyche one iota. I don't think about anything except myself."

That's an animal! Do you know what we want from a human being? Total consideration of his or her environment twenty-four hours a day, never causing destruction, never causing harm, never causing sorrow, distress, pain, *never!* Constant consideration.

During the *Aseres Yemei Teshuvah, bachurim* become terrific *masmidim.* A *bachur* is up till two in the morning learning. Then he goes up to his dormitory to sleep. Two of his colleagues are already sleeping. It's very dark in the room. He wants to put on the light to find his way. Don't you dare put on the light. Don't you dare awaken any of the others from their sleep. Bash your head, but don't bash anyone else's head. You're a mensch. If you're a *chayah*, an animal, switch on the light and don't care about anyone else's pain.

A husband wakes up in the middle of the night. He's thirsty. Okay, so go to the kitchen and take a glass of water, but on your way don't you dare put on your shoes, which will make noise. You might wake up your wife. You're not the only one in the world. In the kitchen, don't put on the light, because you'll awaken your children. "But I can't find my way properly." So don't find your way. Suffer and don't cause suffering to anyone else. Otherwise, you're an animal; we don't see that you're a mensch.

The Creator chose, of all possible *sheluchim* to commit this act of punishment on this earth, which nation? *Bnei Yishmael.* What does the *pasuk* say about this nation? "*V'hu yiheyeh pere adam.*" What does *pere adam* mean? He has a human brain. He can devise the most devious plans. This is why they destroyed the Twin Towers on a daytime flight and not through a nighttime flight, which would have spared thousands of lives, widows, and orphans.

I came to Eretz Yisrael over fifty years ago. A few weeks after I arrived a Jew unintentionally strayed into an Arab village. An Arab grabbed him and stabbed him to death. Eventually they had to return the body to the family for burial. The family noticed that one of his fingers was missing. The widow explained that he had had a ring on that finger. This Arab wanted the ring. All right, so shlep it off. No, it's too much effort. He cut off the finger and brought it home. He showed it to his wife. "Here's the finger with the ring."

I said to the person who told me the story, "These are menschen? These are beasts!"

He said to me, "*Pere adam.*"

I heard this already more than fifty years ago.

The Creator is demanding of us to do *teshuvah* on this *middah.* We have to become people who are living in total, constant consideration of our environment, never to cause destruction or damage to any inert object, vegetation, animal, or human being. Never. You don't wake anyone up, you don't disturb anyone, you don't scare anyone, you don't abuse anyone, and you take one word out of your vocabulary — *selfish* — and get rid of it. You're not the only one in the world, and that is the alef-beis of the human being with *derech eretz*. If you don't have that alef-beis, you are more or less an animal — a two-legged animal perhaps, but an animal. And the Creator is particular about that.

Take a look at the drivers on the road. They drive without any consideration for anyone else. They think they're the only ones on the road, and everyone had better get out of their way.

We are going to have to return to being menschen, human beings, never, ever causing any sorrow or harm to anyone else, not in the morning and not in the evening and not in shul.

Someone told me, after I spoke Friday night somewhere on this topic, "You know, this is the first decent speech I've heard about this whole business. I've heard speakers talk all kinds of nonsense, that our children should not be scared by all this, that we have to tell them that most airplanes don't crash and most buildings are safe. Bush is beefing up the FBI, and we have to beef up our children not to be scared of flying on an airplane." I wonder what else they've been talking about?

There is a *gevaldik limud* to be learned here. The Creator wants a mensch, but from *klal Yisrael* He wants more than menschen. The alef-beis of a civilized human being is total consideration of his fellow man and his environment always. *Derech eretz*. From *klal Yisrael* the Almighty wants a Yid — someone who encourages, helps, uplifts, and brings gladness of heart to every other Yid. Rav Chaim Volozhiner would often say to his son, "The purpose of man in this world is to live, not for his own purposes, but rather to benefit others, in every possible way!"

Let us work on this noble project – smiling at others, greeting them cheerfully, encouraging, forgiving, and comforting. Bringing gladness to the Almighty's world. Let us be the antidote to the *pere adam*. Let us hasten the day of the *geulah*.

## RABBI REUVEN FEINSTEIN

ROSH YESHIVAH, YESHIVA OF STATEN ISLAND, NEW YORK
*From an address at the Agudah Convention (November 22, 2001)*

Before September 11, we felt secure as all the Americans felt secure. We forgot we're in *galus*, something that our ancestors never forgot. We thought of America as a *malchus shel chessed* that lets us pretend we are the same as they and equal to them, when, in truth, we are here by virtue of their goodwill. But with the attack on the World Trade Center, that security was shattered, and we were suddenly awakened to reality. So what should our *hashkafah* be now?

The *Sifri* breaks up the *pasuk* "*Tamim tiheyeh im Hashem Elokecha*" in *parashas Shoftim* into two parts: "*K'she'atah tam*," then "*chelkecha im Hashem Elokecha*." If you are a *tamim*, then you have a *chelek*, portion, with HaKadosh Baruch Hu. The Malbim explains, if you are a *tamim* and refrain from projecting the future – even in permissible ways – and you rely only on Hashem, then you feel *hashgachah pratis*. But if you don't, then *hashgachah pratis* doesn't apply to you. Then you're just like all the rest of the people in the world – things will happen according to the "odds." If you want *hashgachah pratis* to apply to you, you have to have a *chelek* with Hashem.

I want to give an idea of what the Malbim means by that – having a "*chelek* with Hashem." The relationship between the *Ribbono shel olam* and *klal Yisrael* is called "*Elokus*," Godliness. Avraham Avinu made several covenants with HaKadosh Baruch Hu. The *Ribbono shel olam* promised him land and children, but He didn't yet promise him a relationship of *Elokus*. Avraham first had this special relationship with Hashem when he was ninety-nine years old and the *Ribbono shel olam* said to him, "*His'haleich lefanai v'heyei samim.*" Until then, there was no such relationship.

You can see that there is a concept of a tzaddik being deserving of reward. (Noach also made a bris with HaKadosh Baruch Hu – but there was no *Elokus*, no declaration that Noach would be part of His nation and that Hashem would be his God. *Elokus* exists only between Hashem and those who comprehend the true meaning of "*tamim tiheyeh.*") Through this bris with Avraham the *Ribbono shel olam* perpetuated the relationship of *Elokus* with Avraham's children. This means that every one of us is included in "*his'haleich lefanai.*"

I would say that the big *nisayon*, test, of September 11 was whether we are doing our part in this bris of *Elokus*.

There are many opinions on what was the *nisayon* of the *akeidah*. I would like to add another one. The Rambam (*Hilchos Teshuvah* 10:2) says that Avraham Avinu is referred to as "*ahuvi*," my beloved, because he had a sense of the *emes* of HaKadosh Baruch Hu. Because of this sense of truth, he believed in Hashem. If the *akeidah* was a human sacrifice — something that was *sheker* — how could he believe in it? The whole relationship he had with HaKadosh Baruch Hu was based on *emes*. If he now misinterpreted the concept of *emes*, what was the value of the whole relationship until now?

But that's what trust means. Real trust means "I don't understand, but I trust in Hashem that there won't be any hint of *sheker* in His command. Somehow this won't happen. How it won't happen, I don't understand."

What did happen? The *Ribbono shel olam* said, "I asked you to bring him up as an *olah*. I didn't ask you to sacrifice him."

The belief that it can't possibly be wrong is the belief that what comes from the *Ribbono shel olam* is *emes*. Although it may seem *sheker*, we know it's *emes*. That's the *nisayon* of trust. And that's what the *Ribbono shel olam* wants from us.

The question is, how can we bring it from the potential to the actual, to expunge the fear so that we can believe in "*tamim tiheyeh*"? The Gemara says we have to train ourselves. If you walk over to a Yid and ask him, "How do you feel?" he immediately says, "*Baruch Hashem*," or "*Im yirtzeh Hashem*," or "*B'ezras Hashem*." It's appropriate to acknowledge HaKadosh Baruch Hu, and this becomes so much a part of a Jew's speech that he reacts in the proper places with the proper expressions.

The Gemara (*Berachos* 60) says the same thing applies with *bitachon*. You have to train yourself to say, "*Kol d'avid Rachmana l'tav avid* — Everything Hashem does is for good," whenever something happens. If you say it enough, you come to believe it and feel it.

But there's yet another level.

There's a concept of *"Gam zu l'tovah* — This is also for good." A lot of people mix up the two expressions, and the reason is that both come from the same opinion, from Nachum Ish Gam Zu. What is the difference between these two expressions?

*"Kol d'avid..."* is said when there's pain. Rabbi Akiva once came to a town and wanted to find a place to spend the night. Since no one invited him, he stayed in the woods. There his donkey ran away, his rooster was devoured, and his candle kept blowing out. It hurt. It was an uncomfortable night. The next morning, when the whole town was wiped out and he was saved, he was able to say, *"Kol d'avid...."* But it hurt. It could have been done without any pain. It could have happened that he would have had to stay for a bris in the previous town and slept in a mansion, and people would have escorted him to this place. It didn't have to be this way.

*"Gam zu l'tovah"* is reflected in the story of Nachum Ish Gam Zu when he acted as a messenger to bring a box of jewels to bribe the king of Rome. At the inn where he stayed, the jewels were stolen, and the box was filled with sand. When he came to the king, and they opened the box and saw the sand, the king was very upset. Nachum said, *"Gam zu l'tovah."* Eliyahu HaNavi, who was at his side, told the king, "This could be the sand that Avraham used against Kedarla'omer." Nachum Ish Gam Zu's sand became missiles and chariots, which the king employed, and Rome won the next war. The king rewarded the Jews by refilling the box with fancy jewels, and he became a good friend of *klal Yisrael.*

That was good — it was never bad. On the contrary, if Nachum Ish Gam Zu had gone to the king with the jewels, what would have happened? He would have been taking a chance. Even if the king had accepted them, would he have listened to Nachum Ish Gam Zu? As it happened, Nachum Ish Gam Zu came back with jewels, and there was also *shalom.*

When something bad happens, a person is supposed to say, "*Gam zu l'tovah.*" A person has lost his job, yet this could be the best thing that ever happened to him. Until now he was afraid to make a move and go out on his own. After being forced into it, he starts a new business venture and becomes wealthy. On this one would say, "*Gam zu l'tovah.*" Who says it's bad? It may look bad, but you don't know if it's bad.

On the other hand, if someone is out of work for six or eight months, he says, "*Kol d'avid....*" This is for when it really hurts.

This is the level of *bitachon* we must reach.

## RABBI LEVI YITZCHOK HOROWITZ

*THE BOSTONER REBBE*
*From "Coming to Terms with the Trade Center Tragedy"*
*(The Jewish Observer, October 2001)*

The Twin Towers of the World Trade Center represented one of the most colossal monuments to man's material achievements, a collaborative effort of our generation to strive for permanence. And when those towers collapsed like a house of cards, the world gasped in disbelief. In one of the prayers of the *Yamim Nora'im*, we say, "A man's origin is from dust. He is likened to a broken shard, to a withering grass, to a fading flower, to a passing shade, to a dissipating cloud, to the blowing wind, to the flying dust, and to a momentary dream."

Viewing permanence gives us weaklings the inspiration to seek our own greatness, to build skyscrapers, to marvel at their existence and prominence on the skyline. And when one of them is destroyed, we are rudely reminded how weak and transient we are.

The lesson we learn from this disaster is that, as humans, we must acknowledge God's supremacy over all the material world. We must focus on the spiritual side of life, feeding the soul with the study of Torah and the performance of mitzvos.

We humans strive for eternity. This is most dramatically played out in our having and raising children. They are a part of us, and they extend us in time to another generation. On and on.

As Jews, we understand that true immortality and permanence are achieved only by attaching ourselves to God. As we exercise our spiritual nature to fulfill the will of the Almighty through prayers, the study of Torah, and acts of kindness, we build true permanence into our world — by feeding the soul, the only part of us that is capable of reaching eternity. As we reflect on the evil of terrorism and the destruction of the World Trade Center, it is essential to focus on the concept that good is more powerful than evil, that each of us has a greater power to build and to heal, much more so than those who might succeed in destroying and killing. And we exercise our power of good through our acts of kindness, not only toward our fellow Jews, but also to all peoples of the world. These acts of kindness represent walking in the ways of God.

Chazal tell us that the force for good is five hundred times stronger than the power of evil. If evil by the hands of a few people can create so much suffering, pain, and devastation, just think how much more opportunity there is for the multitude to do good, to move in the opposite direction from evil: comforting, healing, and building. Each and every one of us possesses such a great potential for good to contribute to civilization and the world. This is a powerful message. We are therefore the bearers of not just a good message but of an action plan to build a better world. Our inadequate feelings and emotions have to be put aside at times in order to direct our energies to creating a better world through building a better community, a better family, a better self, through attaching ourselves to our Creator.

# RABBI SHMUEL KAMENETSKY

*ROSH YESHIVAH, YESHIVA OF PHILADELPHIA*
*Excerpted from an address at the Convention of Agudath Israel of America*
*(November 22, 2001)*

These are turbulent days, extraordinary days. There was a statement made a little while ago that things will never be the same. The question is, will *we* remain the same?

Things will not be the same, that's for sure. Those beautiful buildings that portrayed American glory, the Twin Towers, overlooking the Statute of Liberty with her outstretched arm, accepting people from all over, where thousands of people were lost, thousands of *neshamos* lost, orphans, widows. It changed the world. I go outside and look at a plane, and I think, *Is this a mashchis? A vehicle, a plane, that can go from one place to another, can become a mashchis?*

Someone called me right after the incident and asked me what he should say to people. I told him something I heard in the name of the Klausenberger Rebbe, *zt"l*. They asked him in the concentration camp, "Where was God?" That was after the Rebbe had lost his family, his wife and children. The Rebbe answered, "Could this have happened without God? Only the *Ribbono shel olam* could do something like this. Is this a normal thing? It's abnormal. It must be the Hand of Hashem."

This was his *emunah*, his faith. That's what he saw in every incident. The Chafetz Chaim said that we have to pay heed to an earthquake in China. We have to listen. We have to question, "What kind of message does it convey to the Jews?"

After seeing the *middas hadin* — and this is a time of *middas hadin* — we have to remember those who died this year, *geonim*, tzaddikim: Rav Gifter, *zt"l*; Rav Avigdor Miller, *zt"l*; Rav Pam, *zt"l*; Rav Shach, *zt"l*. All had such an impact on thousands of people. The *Ribbono shel olam* is showing us something. He is teaching us that everything is in His Hands. He took away these *gedolim* now. Perhaps we relied on them. These are the ones who were protecting the whole world. The *Ribbono shel olam* said, "We'll see what you will do without them." What we lived through now gives us a glimpse of this *middas hadin*.

The Seforno says that Yaakov Avinu accepted upon himself *middas hadin*. Chazal tell us that when Moshe Rabbeinu saw Rabbi Akiva being raked with iron combs, he was told that this was *middas hadin*. The world was originally intended to exist with *middas hadin* but ultimately could not exist without *middas harachamim*. In every generation, tzaddikim have taken it upon themselves to live only with *middas hadin*. This is the highest level.

The *Da'as Tevunos* says a person is required to ask, "What did the *Avos* do to merit the *Ribbono shel olam*'s love? What did Moshe Rabbeinu do?" But how can we compare ourselves to them?

A person is required to strive for greater heights in doing the will of the Creator. We are supposed to do more and more. Whatever we do must not be enough for us. We must force ourselves to do more mitzvos and more *chassadim*. The *Avos* always strived to do better, to go further, to reach higher levels. A person is required to do more than he thinks he can, to elevate himself. If he doesn't, he is missing the chance.

The Kotzker asked his *talmidim*, "Which one is on a higher level, the one who is at the top of the ladder or the one at the bottom?" He explained that it is the one who is at the bottom who is on a higher level, because he strives to raise himself up. That's exactly what we have to do.

# RABBI CHAIM DOV KELLER

*ROSH YESHIVAH, TELSHE OF CHICAGO*
*From an address (September 12, 2001)*

We are living through *yamim nora'im*, awesome and fearful days. We need a prophet to explain to us what has happened, not to mention what will happen.

It has been a year of *tzaros*. We said in the Selichos this morning, "*Me'eis l'eis tzarasi merubah miyom she'avar kashah haba* — From moment to moment my troubles increase; the day that comes is more difficult than the one that passed." We have lived through a year of troubles and suffering for the Jewish people as a whole and for countless individuals.

It has been obvious for many months that we are living in a time of divine wrath. It appears that the *Ribbono shel olam* is not satisfied with His world. There are wars, famine, and sickness all over the world, and we have suffered especially in Eretz Yisrael from daily casualties. In America we lulled ourselves until now into the belief that we are secure. But the events of these last days have left us stunned.

The Rambam tells us that even though the mitzvah of shofar is an inscrutable divine decree, it signals to us, "*Uru yesheinim mishnaschem...* — Wake up, those of you who sleep, and those of you who have fallen into a deep slumber, arouse yourself from your slumber." If we have not heard the message of the shofar of Elul, then we surely must hear the awesome message the *Ribbono shel olam* has sounded with His shofar. He has given us the message that no place is safe, that no one here on earth is in control. You've built yourselves towers. You call them the World Trade Center. It's not there anymore.

The world's greatest military power is the United States. Its power is centered in the Pentagon. The Pentagon has been hit, and no one has any idea of what the future will bring. Only He is the *Ba'al habayis*. The *Ribbono shel olam* is teaching us that He is in charge, that no human power controls the world.

In the Second World War there were a number of great powers: the United States, Russia, England, China, France, Germany, Japan. But one by one they weakened. The only superpower left was the United States, and now we see that the United States can be struck by a few crazy men. Do you think these *meshugaim* and countless others like them who would destroy the world have not been around for a long time? You think these people just appeared now?

The Vilna Gaon comments on the passage in the Haggadah "*Shebechol dor vador omdim aleinu l'chaloseinu v'HaKadosh Baruch Hu matzileinu miyadam* — In every generation there are those who rise up to destroy us, and the Holy One, blessed be He, saves us from their hands." You think there's no one there who wants to destroy *klal Yisrael*? he says. "*Tzei u'lemad...* — Go out and learn from Lavan HaArami." Lavan sought to destroy the entire world. Yaakov was living with him; Lavan was his father-in-law, his uncle, his business partner. Yaakov had no inkling that Lavan wanted to destroy him. But he did.

These people have been around all along.

Even if we didn't know who they were or what they intended, they were there. But they couldn't do anything if the Ruler of the universe wouldn't let them. If the *Ribbono shel olam* is not happy, each of us has to say, "What can I do to make the *Ribbono shel olam* pleased with His world?"

We see what a *churban* a few individuals can cause. We're not talking about armies with superweapons. It is said they used plastic knives and box cutters. No one will ever really know. But look what *yechidim* accomplished. And there are thousands, millions, of such individuals. If the *Ribbono shel*

*olam* would open our eyes to see the number of would-be destroyers in the world, we wouldn't be able to survive from the
terror we'd feel. Hashem constantly guards and protects
Yisrael and the world. But when He is not satisfied, a few individuals can do the most horrific things.

"*Merubah middah tovah mimiddas puraniyus* — The divine
measure of good is much greater than that of punishment." Individuals have such a great potential to do good in this world.
Moshe Rabbeinu alone saved *klal Yisrael* with his *tefillos*. We,
too, must all strengthen ourselves with our *tefillos* for all of
*klal Yisrael* and pray for the safety and security of this great
country.

This is the time of *chevlei Mashiach*. Our Sages tell us, "*Mah
ya'aseh adam viyenatzel michevlo shel Mashiach ya'asok
baTorah u'vigemilus chassadim* — What should a person do to
save himself from the birth pangs and suffering that will pre-
cede the coming of Mashiach? He should engage in Torah
study and in acts of kindness." There are those who say that
the Second World War was the culmination of the *chevlei
Mashiach*. No one knows. But the events of the past days
surely have all the signs of a time of terrible suffering, and
each person has to seek some merit to be saved from this suffering.

*Bnei Torah*, students of the yeshivah, have a special responsibility. The first *Rashi* in Tanach cites our Sages' statement that the world was created for the sake of Torah and for
the sake of Yisrael. If there are no Jewish people learning Torah, the world will cease to exist. And in direct proportion to
the quantity and quality of Torah learning, there will be a se-

cure perpetuation of the Almighty's creation. These are days that call for greatness, and we cannot be small people. We are facing a war. The war will be fought with all sorts of weapons with awesome capacity for destruction.

But there is another war, on a higher spiritual level, that will be the decisive factor in the victory or, Heaven forbid, the defeat of the forces of good against the forces of evil. The weapons in that war are Torah and *tefillah* and *gemilus chassadim*, acts of kindness. Torah study in the yeshivah must be strengthened with no interruptions. Our *tefillos* have to be said with greater concentration. And we must put our minds and hearts to find ways of helping others.

Finally, each person must ask himself, "What is the meaning of life? What do I want from my life?" When we let the events embodied by the words "World Trade Center" sink in, when we have seen what has happened to what was called the World Trade Center, when we think of the thousands of lives lost, when we think of the widows and the orphans, the *agunos*, the parents, relatives, and friends of all these people, there must be a sobering reassessment of what life is all about. One minute a person was the head of a large, successful company, and now that person and that company no longer exist.

Each Jew, especially each *ben Torah*, must think, *What can I do now? How can I reorder my priorities so that the Ribbono shel olam will once again be happy with His world?* I must think, "*Yehi chevod Hashem l'olam yismach Hashem b'ma'asav* — Let the glory of Hashem be eternal, and let Hashem rejoice with his creatures." Let this be a *shenas ratzon*, a year of divine favor. A year of doing what the *Ribbono shel olam* wants. It does not matter what this or that country thinks, nor what the opinion polls think, nor what the talk shows think. It's what the *Ribbono shel olam* thinks that's important.

Each of us must say to himself: What do I want to accomplish in my life? Is my object in life to have a good time, to have a lot of money, to have a high position, to have a big company that can go up in smoke? Or is it to sanctify the Name of Hashem? And how can I sanctify the Name of Hashem? By Torah and acts of *chessed*.

We should pray to the *Ribbono shel olam*, "*Bnei ircha kimei olam v'rapei mizbechacha heichal v'ulam Yehudah v'Yisrael sham ya'avducha kulam yigdal shimcha mei'olam v'ad olam* — Rebuild your city as it was in days of yore and rebuild the Beis HaMikdash. Let the people of Israel all serve You there together, and let Your Name be made great for all eternity."

# RABBI YAAKOV PERLOW

*THE NOVOMINSKER REBBE,*
*ROSH AGUDATH ISRAEL OF AMERICA*
From his address at the Agudah Convention (November 22, 2001)

This is not an ordinary convention of Agudath Israel. These are not ordinary times. The last two and a half months have opened a new phase in our lives, a new period of Jewish and world history. Whoever doesn't see this has very limited vision. Our challenge now is to understand the meaning of the change that has occurred and its message to Torah Jews.

The theme of this convention is *"She'al Avicha V'Yagedcha."* The previous words in that *pasuk* say, *"Binu shenos dor v'dor"*

— we should assess what current events are teaching us.

We have suddenly been shown the deadly reach of Yishmael, whom the *Rishonim* and the *mekubalim* say is even more dangerous than Esav. Before our eyes, a successful attack was made on society itself and on the symbols of world stability. The United States government, the military, all of us seem helpless. We don't know what to expect tomorrow. We don't feel safe anymore opening an envelope that came in the mail. And many lives have been lost this past year in Eretz Yisrael, victims of Yishmael's terror.

As *ma'aminim*, believers, we should be stunned and worried about the passing of tzaddikim. We are still in the *sheloshim* of the passing of Rav Shach, *zt"l*, and we still feel the passing away of other *gedolei Yisrael* this past year. This ought to shake us up and make us heed the last few words of *masseches Sanhedrin*: "*Tzaddik niftar min ha'olam ra'ah ba l'olam....*" — "When a righteous person dies, evil enters the world...." The *gemara* there quotes and explains the *pasuk* "The righteous die, and no one takes it to heart, and pious men are taken away without anyone considering that the tzaddik is taken away before the evil occurs" (*Yeshayahu* 57:1). The Gemara understands this to mean — and Rashi explains it this way in his commentary on the *pasuk* — that people do not realize that the death of tzaddikim is a foreboding of coming misfortune, Heaven forbid.

All this is very worrisome. The Torah gives us ominous signs about the days before Mashiach that frightened even Chazal themselves. All the signs of the present should make us deeply fear the future, but in order to invoke and bring about the *rachamim* and *chassadim* that we pray for, in order to influence the conduct of HaKadosh Baruch Hu and change it from *din* to *rachamim*, we must first understand that the current events contain teachings and lessons for all of us.

It is obvious by now that Hashem is shaking up the great citadels of civilization. The prophecy in the second chapter of *Yeshayah* about the judgment of HaKadosh Baruch Hu preceding the end of days says that Hashem will have a day of retribution against every proud and arrogant person, who will be brought low. That day of retribution will extend to all the "cedars of Lebanon and all the oaks of Bashan and all the lofty mountains and all the exalted hills and against every tall tower and against every fortified wall and against the ships of Tarshish and the splendid palaces." The *pasuk* goes on to state the climax, that the haughtiness of humans will be humbled; the arrogance of man will be brought down. Hashem alone will be exalted on that day. All the proud products of human prowess, the heights of earthly existence, are metaphors for the arrogance of man, which will be reduced and humbled.

If we see the collapse of the Twin Towers as a blow to the bricks and mortar of society, to its technology and commerce, to its power and might — and it was certainly all of that — the *navi* conveys to us the ultimate message. It was meant to humble the haughtiness of man, to shame his arrogance so that it remain boldly clear: "*V'nisgav Hashem levado bayom hahu* — God alone will be exalted on that day." This, my friends, is the simple, clear, true lesson to be learned from the events that have befallen us.

These events are warning signals of further judgment.

They should frighten us to the bone. However, like all forms of *middas hadin*, they can become building blocks to a better inner world, a wake-up call for *teshuvah*, for moral improvement, as the *pasuk* says, "*Tosheiv enosh ad daka vatomar shuvu bnei adam* — You return man to dust, and you say, 'Repent, children of man.' " These events can have a constructive, therapeutic effect on our lives and our future and cause HaKadosh Baruch Hu to rise from the seat of *din* and be seated on the seat of *rachamim*.

My friends, we must respond. We must change, because everything else has changed. And the changes must take place in those very areas that reflect *gei'us ha'adam, ram anashim*, in the symbols of arrogance and affluence, in the symbols of power and possession. We must make every effort to return to the simple, true virtues of life, of Jewish life, of Torah life. We must rid ourselves of the excess baggage impacting upon our behavior and our *neshamos* that expresses *gei'us ha'adam*.

On Yom Kippur, when reciting *vidui* and praying *ne'ilah*, when we stand helpless before Hashem like a beggar at the door, we feel deeply, truly, David HaMelech's words: "*V'anochi tola'as v'lo ish cherpas adam u'vezui am* — I am a worm and not a man, a man of shame, disgraced among the nation." We feel Avraham Avinu's words, "*V'anochi afar v'eifer* — I am but dust and ashes." We are overtaken with humility, with a sense of our nothingness. Why do we feel it only then? Because on Yom Kippur we are honest with ourselves. We are not beholden to our egos. The *yetzer* in us is subdued. We shut him out of our thoughts.

My friends, today the Master of the universe is sending us

signals that we'd better shape up and extend our Yom Kippur thoughts to the rest of the year. If the shofar thunders in the city, do people not tremble? If disaster occurs in the city, is it not Hashem's doing? asks the prophet Amos. The simple question for us is, how do we Torah Jews begin to internalize Yom Kippur thoughts and manifest them in our behavior? All the *mussar* in the world will not make us change unless we begin somewhere – in the externals of our lifestyle, which will then effect an internal search, a quest for self-betterment.

In this troublesome time, when we are trying to recover from a calamity at our doorstep, when our brothers in Eretz Yisrael are in danger each day, with so many *korbanos* this past year, a time when so many among us are without *parnassah*, there is so much financial stress and strain, now – especially now – is the time to revise the way we live, to practice restraint, to curb envy, to curb conspicuous consumption, and to exhibit the virtues of modesty and simplicity that should define the lifestyle of Torah Jews.

I return to a familiar theme: downsizing the cost and character of our *simchah*s, particularly weddings. Aside from its moral perspective, the prospect of making an expensive, elaborate *chasunah* is a heavy burden weighing down countless families in our community and sending them into steep debt. It is absolutely wrong, unjust, for people to suffer hardship and debt for years because they had to keep up with their neighbors or their friends in shul, spending many thousands of dollars on one, two, or three weddings they can ill afford. It's almost criminal, and it's got to stop! This problem has been discussed for many years at these conventions and elsewhere, but now is the time to act.

"*Yisrael kedoshim heim* — The Jewish people are holy." It is a tribute that a group of community leaders with a sense of mission for the benefit of the public have spearheaded a drive, joined by hundreds of families of reasonable means. Guidelines and parameters have been formulated. These guidelines, self-imposed by the community itself, will hopefully and finally change the character and cost of a *Yiddishe simchah*. The guidelines follow in the path and the spirit of *takanos* of earlier generations, dating back to the Va'ad Arba Aratzos, when the *gedolei hador* placed rules and limitations on all kinds of festivities.

We must all understand that the purpose of attending a *chasunah* is to bring joy to the *chasan* and *kallah*, not to eat a piece of chicken and stand at the bar. We must also understand that the Torah concept of *simchah* does not include lavishness in food, music, flowers, and huge expenditures on gifts and garments. This is the kind of tradition we can do without. A *Yiddishe simchah* should be festive but not ostentatious, joyous but understated — a *simchah*, not a party.

Yes, it will require a new mindset on the part of many, some drastic changes in our habits. And we can also expect some protest, some opposition, some disagreement. It will not be easy. But if *Yiddishkeit* is the criterion for how we live our lives, these changes will uplift all of us. They will be a pride to our community, a profound *zechus harabbim*, and a *kiddush Hashem* of the highest order. Hopefully this convention will see some culmination of these efforts.

We must also remember that the past and the meaning of

"*V'nikdashti besoch bnei Yisrael* — I will be sanctified among the children of Israel" is critically important at this time. When *kevod Shamayim* is dragged through the gutter, when blatant anti-Semitism is given free rein, when there is danger for all of us in Eretz Yisrael and elsewhere, and no one knows what the future holds, there is no greater *zechus* than to proclaim *malchus Shamayim* at every living moment. What is, after all, the purpose of HaKadosh Baruch Hu in creation if not the revelation and expression of His Kingship here on earth? If so, our behavior toward this end will testify openly that we are a worthwhile instrument in Hashem's design and that we are worth keeping alive.

I mentioned recently on another occasion that it is now more important than ever to seek out opportunities of *kiddush shem Shamayim*, to consciously create a *kiddush shem Shamayim*, and certainly to avoid any semblance of *chillul shem Shamayim* — to proclaim through our behavior before the gentiles and among ourselves that "*Hashem Hu haElokim* — Hashem, He is God.*" There is only one purpose for all of existence, one ultimate truth: "*Hashem Hu haElokim.*"

This is to be the barometer of our entire daily routine, the criterion for our actions at every moment. This ought to be the ever-present question in our minds at all times: Does what I am doing testify that "*Hashem Hu haElokim*"? It is a formidable task to be constantly, consciously concerned with *kiddush shem Shamayim*, but this is what I believe we need to do at this critical juncture — to increase *kevod Shamayim* at every turn. If we fulfill this sacred task, we will have been true to our sacred mission: "*U'varuch shem kevodo l'olam v'yimalei chevodo es kol ha'aretz amen v'amen* — Blessed is His glorious Name forever and may all the earth be filled with His glory."

## RABBI YECHIEL YITZCHOK PERR

*ROSH YESHIVAH, YESHIVA OF FAR ROCKAWAY, NEW YORK*

On September 11 a new seriousness descended on the Western World. The events of that day were a wake-up call to abandon the childishness of our previous lives, the superficiality of our former goals. On that day the theaters were empty — Broadway was in chaos. The mayor appealed to people to go back to the theaters. The actors and actresses were putting on shows in the streets, trying to entice the populace back to the theaters and to their mindless entertainment.

But the people were not going. The reality of September 11 had blown away the mindless chatter and emptiness that was their culture. It was a great tragedy that revealed the core of another tragedy — the tragedy of a society that was totally unprepared to think a serious thought, to live a life that could have meaning.

September 11 taught the emptiness of the world around us. We have to make up our minds to stop peeking longingly at the outer world, wishing we could be part of it, join it. The outer world is a world of silly children. It cannot coexist with the reality of life in the larger world, and it cannot coexist with the seriousness of life of the private individual.

In this way, September 11 has been a defining moment for Western culture. We Torah Jews should use the experience of that day to strengthen our obstinacy and to build higher our walls against the mindlessness of the society in which we find ourselves.

## RABBI YISROEL RAKOWSKY

*ROSH YESHIVAH, OHR SOMAYACH, MONSEY, NEW YORK*
*From an address given before Yom Kippur 5762*

W e are not going to interpret the events and make predictions. We just want to understand how a Yid who believes in HaKadosh Baruch Hu and in the Torah is supposed to react to such an occurrence and what he is supposed to do.

The Rambam writes in *Hilchos Ta'aniyos* that there is a positive commandment in the Torah to do two things when a calamity strikes the community: to cry out in *tefillah* to *HaKadosh Baruch Hu* and to sound the trumpets. (The Magen Avraham, in *Hilchos Ta'anis*, explains why the mitzvah of blowing the trumpets does not apply anymore, but that is a halachic matter.) This is one of the ways to do *teshuvah* — when a *tzarah* befalls *klal Yisrael*, and they cry out because of the *tzarah*, it is our responsibility to make everyone aware that *tzaros* come upon *klal Yisrael* or upon the world because of their iniquities, as the *pasuk* says, "It is because of your sins." That is the only thing that will remove the *tzarah*.

But if they will not cry out and people will say this is a natural occurrence — that the fanatics who did it were crazy, it just happened, and it has nothing to do with me — they are not seeing it the way they should. HaKadosh Baruch Hu is the One

Who brought the *tzarah*. He wants us to recognize that he is the King of the world. He gave us a sign that He is running the world, and I say that it has nothing to do with me, that it just happened?

"And it caused them to cleave to their bad ways" — this verse means that the tragedy doesn't change the person in any way. He remains the same. This *tzarah* will, *chas v'shalom*, bring other *tzaros*. He wants us to recognize that when He brings *tzaros* it is because of *aveiros* and we should do *teshuvah*.

The Rambam tells us very clearly what our reaction and our attitude should be in the face of tragedy. We must recognize that whatever happened is from *yad Hashem*. Many people perished in this disaster, and many were miraculously saved. On each one there was a *gezar din*, a Heavenly judgment, deciding whether he should be there or should not be there and be saved.

I spoke to my nephew who worked in that building. Usually, at eight-thirty in the morning, when he arrived at work, there were people in his office. That day no one was there. But something else happened. He had an appointment in San Francisco and was supposed to be there Tuesday night and Wednesday morning. Tuesday morning he had a ticket for the flight that was to fly from Newark to San Francisco. He had told someone the day before that he wasn't sure if he would leave Tuesday morning or push it off till Tuesday afternoon. At the last minute he decided to go to Selichos in the morning and take a Tuesday evening flight. That Tuesday morning flight was the plane that crashed in Pennsylvania.

Every single person who worked in that building or was in that neighborhood or was in that plane, we have to believe with complete faith that his destiny was decreed from Above. We are not saying it was worthwhile — we are taking the lesson that we're supposed to take, that there's nothing that happens in this world at random. A person does not stub his finger down here unless it has been ordained in Heaven that this is what has to happen. Even more so, in such a calamity, which shattered so many families, a *gezar din* was passed on every one of them. We cannot understand the ways of Hashem, but at least we should understand that it is a message that HaKadosh Baruch Hu is sending us.

In 1914, when the First World War broke out, the Chafetz Chaim wrote that the great upheaval affected the whole world and all the Jewish people — physically and spiritually. He would have written similarly about these events.

There is no doubt that this a wake-up call from Heaven, he wrote, that we should return to HaKadosh Baruch Hu, as it says in the Torah that when things will be tight, and the things mentioned in *parashas Ki Savo* will happen to you, you should turn to HaKadosh Baruch Hu. Everyone has an obligation to cry out and ask Him to help us, and we should pray for our government that it should be successful in this war.

We might say, "So it's a war. So what? What does it have to do with me? No one was drafted here from my *shtiebel*, so what's the problem?" Heaven forbid, continues the Chafetz Chaim, that we should sit with our hands folded and say, "It doesn't affect me directly. I'm twenty miles from the World Trade Center. I don't have any relatives who were there." We have to employ the "profession" of our ancestors and cry out to Hashem, because we have to recognize that everything is dependent on Him, as it says in *Amos*, "Is it possible that there should be a calamity in a city and Hashem did not do it?" If there is a calamity, says the *navi*, it means that Hashem did it. It wasn't just some crazy man who decided, "You know what? I'm going to crash into the Twin Towers." No, it was ordained by Hashem that for some reason this calamity had to strike the city of New York and the country.

When tragedy occurs and Jews are directly affected by it, how much more so do we have to cry out to HaKadosh Baruch Hu. The Chafetz Chaim says we have certain obligations to the host country in which we have been given the right to live. America has been good to the Jewish people. When it is under attack, we have to pray that HaKadosh Baruch Hu will help the leaders of this country to fight the enemy. As Yirmeyahu writes, "Look out and seek the peace of the city in which you live." How can we sit complacently? We have to pray that He help the government and His people.

The Chafetz Chaim goes on to say that he was surprised each city hadn't proclaimed a fast day when World War I broke out. It is also interesting that the Chafetz Chaim didn't try to interpret exactly what was happening in terms of Mashiach. He did, however, write in more than one place about seventy years ago that he was positive that what was happening was part of *ikvesa d'Meshicha*, that we are on the heels of Mashiach. We don't know if it will take another five years, one year, ten years, or fifty years. We are witnessing the events that are leading up to the coming of Mashiach.

The Chafetz Chaim quotes the prophet Yeshayahu, who says that in the days before the arrival of Mashiach we will be like a woman who is having labor pains. Before the great, joyful moment when she bears her child, she goes through very, very difficult labor pains. Just at the moment she thinks she can't take it anymore, that it's too terrible, the baby is born. The Chafetz Chaim says that before Mashiach comes the world has to pay a debt for one reason or another and the accounts are being settled. That is why we have seen so many *tzaros* in this century, both of the *klal* and of individuals. It is a sign of the imminent coming of Mashiach. It is our obligation to believe every day that he's coming and that this is all part of it.

When the sons of Yaakov returned from Egypt to their father and found the money in their sack, what was the first thing they said? They said, "What did HaKadosh Baruch Hu do to us?" When something happens, the first thing a person has to think is *What did HaKadosh Baruch Hu do here?* Nothing happens by chance.

It is very interesting that of all the books of Tanach we read from the book of *Yonah* on Yom Kippur. The story is that the gentile nation of Ninveh had sinned. HaKadosh Baruch Hu told Yonah the prophet to go to the city of Ninveh and admonish the people that if they don't repent the whole city would be destroyed. Yonah did not want to go to rebuke the city. Chazal tell us that he didn't want to go because he felt that if the nations of the world do *teshuvah* when he comes to them with the word of Hashem, it reflects badly on *klal Yisrael*, who have so many wonderful prophets and yet they haven't done *teshuvah*.

So Yonah ran away. But HaKadosh Baruch Hu didn't let him run. He brought him back and sent him to the city of Ninveh to give them *mussar*.

What happened? They started to do *teshuvah*, and they put on sackcloths. Chazal tell us that they changed some of their deeds, but in their hearts they didn't change that much, that they weren't complete *ba'alei teshuvah*. Nevertheless, HaKadosh Baruch Hu saved the city of Ninveh. He spared them and didn't put them to death. Yonah said, "You see, HaKadosh Baruch Hu? I didn't want to go to Ninveh. Now You spared them, and they didn't even do complete *teshuvah*."

Later Yonah was sitting outside, and the sun overhead was too hot. HaKadosh Baruch Hu caused a certain flower to grow, and Yonah enjoyed the plant's shade. Then the flower dried up, and the sun beat down on him again. Yonah felt very bad. The flower was providing him shade, and suddenly the shade went away. HaKadosh Baruch Hu said to Yonah, "Look at you, Yonah. You were disturbed about such a small thing, that this one plant withered. And I should not have compassion on the city of Ninveh, which has more than twelve thousand people? I should destroy all these people? Look how terrible I would feel if all these people were destroyed."

Yonah didn't even make the flower, but HaKadosh Baruch Hu made the people. "It says that I am good to all of creation. Why shouldn't I have mercy on all these people?"

The *navi* is telling us that HaKadosh Baruch Hu has mercy on all the creations of the world. *Klal Yisrael* is His chosen people, and it has a special purpose in this world. Everything that happens in this world, big or small, is because of *klal Yisrael*, but we have to empathize with the *tza'ar* that the world at large experiences, which our country is experiencing now. At the same time, each of us has to look at himself and say, "What can I do to achieve my own personal *teshuvah*?" Each of us should not look only at the big picture but also at himself.

There is no better time than now to make a *cheshbon hanefesh*, to do some introspection, as the Gemara says, "What should man do to save himself from the birth pangs of Mashiach's coming? He should learn Torah and do acts of kindness to others." It doesn't help to listen to the news and to read the newspapers. Each one of us has a tremendous task, to make a *cheshbon hanefesh* to save himself and the rest of the world from *chevlei Mashiach*.

# RABBI AVROHOM YOSEF ROSENBLUM

*ROSH YESHIVAH, SHA'AREI YOSHER, BROOKLYN, NEW YORK*
*Based on an address delivered before Rosh HaShanah 5762*

The world was shaken to the core by the events of September 11. It's obvious that it has a direct connection to *klal Yisrael*, both in Eretz Yisrael and in the diaspora. We are traumatized by the report of the many casualties. Who knows how much they suffered before their souls departed? We should all feel deep sorrow for them.

We need to assess the magnitude of what happened and comprehend, for one thing, how meaningless is materialism. The mighty Twin Towers, the millions of dollars and expertise that went into their construction, collapsed within minutes.

This brings home the lesson that only Torah and mitzvos are enduring. For the Jews who were killed, their wealth, their business, their plans...everything evaporated. What survived were their Torah and mitzvos, which are everlasting and paved their way to Gan Eden. It is obvious that all the material possessions and vanity that accompany man on this earth are valueless in the eyes of the Creator. Within moments, the strongest and richest symbols of the mightiest nation in the world were reduced to rubble by a few Muslim fanatics.

What Hitler and Stalin couldn't accomplish, these few fanatics succeeded in achieving. During the world wars, when 40 million people died, not even a gunshot was heard on American shores. No Russian or Nazi bomb fell here. But these few fanatics immobilized the whole country.

Whoever looked upon this tragedy, in which thousands died such grotesque deaths, impassively, interested only in the news, failing to see the Creator's Hand and His warning signs, unmoved to do *teshuvah*, to learn Torah and perform *ma'asim tovim*, is suffering from *timtum halev* created by his sins. His heart is permeated with impurity. How can he rid himself of this impurity? Through Torah and mitzvos, which create *kedushah* and mellow the heart, and through *teshuvah*.

We have to realize that the event was intended as a lesson for us Jews. *Tzaros* come upon the world to atone for our sins and to open our eyes to see the Creator's hand. If He had not found our deeds lacking, the nations would not be able to cause harm. We need to search within the *tzaros* to see His hand and into the Torah to find ways to fulfill His will.

We have to remember that He loves us and that even in the darkest exile He will never abandon us.

# RABBI MATISYAHU SALOMON

*MASHGIACH OF BETH MEDRASH GOVOHA, LAKEWOOD*
*Address at Kinus Teshuvah (September 15, 2001)*

Over the last few days, Jews all over the world came together to pray for those who were caught up in the terrible tragedy, to feel for those who still don't know what has happened to their nearest and their dearest, and to learn and take lessons on what the Creator so obviously wants us to hear. This *kinus* was not supposed to take place today. It was planned for an earlier time. I believe it is part of *hashgachas Hashem* that it was moved to this particular moment, so that we could come together before Rosh HaShanah. Even without the *tekiah gedolah* that the Creator blew last Tuesday (September 11), we arranged to come together – and this is a wonderful *zechus*. I want to explain to what extent.

In the *sefer Lev Eliyahu*, by my rebbe, Rav Eliyahu Lopian, *zt"l*, there is a piece on *parashas Yisro* with a footnote that says he said this *devar Torah* in the Lakewood Yeshivah about forty-five years ago, in 1956. And this is what he said:

We are in the time that is described as *ikvesa d'Meshicha*, the time preceding the coming of Mashiach. The reason it is called "*ikvesa*," some explain, is because *ikvos* means "footsteps." These are the footsteps of His Mashiach, when the faint sounds of a very, very small tread become a louder and louder march of Mashiach coming closer and closer toward us. It can take a long time, but it's getting closer, and this is what *klal Yisrael* has been hoping for through the ages. We read in *Nevi'im* that in the last moments before the Revelation of the

Creator's Shechinah in *klal Yisrael*, there will be a lot of suffering. We hope that we have already gone through most of it.

What's going to be in the future? Reb Elya said. We don't know. Reb Elya describes how he himself heard at a meeting of *rabbanim*, when the war was looming over everyone's heads, that they were trying to pressure Reb Elchanan, who had just landed in England on his way back from America to Poland, to stay and build a yeshivah there. Why go back when the fires had already begun to burn?

Reb Elya heard Rav Elchanan Wasserman say in the name of the Chafetz Chaim that Chazal say that the War of Gog and Magog, which is the ultimate war, will come in three stages. At that time, when the Chafetz Chaim said this, it was just after the First World War in 1918. He said that the First World War was the first stage of the War of Gog and Magog. In about twenty-five years' time, he said, the second stage would begin. And then would come the third stage – and that would be a terrible tragedy for *klal Yisrael* – and from that would come a salvation.

Rav Elchanan concluded that we will all have to go through the *chevlei Mashiach*; he who is prepared will merit to see the salvation. The British Jews had asked him why he was going back to Poland, with the Germans and the Polish already waging war. Wouldn't it be better to stay in England? He said to them, "What do you think? This is not going to affect you here in England? It's not going to affect the whole world? You think it will happen only in a little corner? Everyone is going to suffer. The question is, who earlier and who later? Therefore I'm going back to my yeshivah."

Reb Elya quotes the verse in *Daniel* that describes what will occur "at that terrible time" (*Daniel* 12:1): When the foundations of the world will totter, when confusion will reign, when legitimate might and power will become insignificant before everyone's eyes — as we see it beginning to happen now — "*klal Yisrael* will be rescued, each one who is written in the book." Which book is it talking about?

Rav Sa'adya Gaon explains, "What does it mean '*kol hanimtza kasuv basefer* — each one who is written in the book"? He says that Malachi, whose prophecies were the last to be written down, when speaking about the end of days describes how Hashem blames *klal Yisrael* saying, "Your words have been strong against Me" (*Malachi* 3:13). And *klal Yisrael* will say, "What did we say against you?" And Hashem answers, "You said, '*Shav avod Elokim* — it isn't worth it to serve God. What benefit did we have from keeping His mitzvos, from not doing *aveiros*? Hashem pushed us away. In fact, we are confirming that the sinners were right. They tested Hashem, and they escaped'" (ibid., 14).

Could you have said that and then turn to Hashem and say, "What did we say? We didn't say anything"? The Alter of Slabodka says a wonderful thing. They didn't actually say those words. They would never have dared to utter such blasphemy. But if a Torah Jew, who represents *Yiddishkeit*, walks down the street, mixes with people, and is obviously not a happy person, if he doesn't show that his life has content, if he is not an example of refinement and fulfillment, then he is shouting to the world, "*Shav avod Elokim* — It isn't worthwhile to serve Hashem."

He is saying to everyone, "We didn't make it, but you made it. You are happy people. You have your entertainment, your pleasures. It seems to me that you have everything, and I go around with my long face." You are telling everyone, "What benefit do we have in keeping His mitzvos? What do we get out of it? It isn't a pleasure. It isn't life itself. It isn't an achievement. I don't feel fulfilled." He is saying to everyone who sees and feels his unhappiness, "*Shav avod Elokim ma betza ki shamarnu mishmarto* — It isn't worth it to serve God; what benefit did we have from keeping His mitzvos?" Hashem seems to have pushed us away, and we seem to be affirming those who do what they want, who extract the pleasures of life and seem to get a better deal. And that's an indictment of Torah observance.

When they received this message from the prophet Malachi, who was speaking about our time, those who feared Hashem said, "What has gone wrong with our lives that Hashem can accuse us of saying, '*Shav avod Elokim*'?" When the God-fearing sit together and try to strengthen one another and they try to find meaning in their lives — when people come together for that purpose — the *Ribbono shel olam* listens in on that discussion. He writes down in a special book all those who fear Him, who come together to seek *chizuk*, who suddenly realize that life has to be much more fulfilling, that we have to represent the *simchah* of Torah and mitzvos.

The verse says, "I am going to keep that book for that special day" (*Malachi* 3:17). Rav Sa'adya Gaon says, "In that terrible time of Gog U'Magog, when Hashem is going to show the world He is the only One in charge and no one can defy Him, they will be the ones who escape. And who are they? The ones who are written down in that *sefer*."

When we stand on Rosh HaShanah and say to Hashem, "*Zachreinu l'chaim melech chafetz bachaim v'kasveinu b'sefer hachaim* — Remember us for life, O King who desires life, and write us down in the Book of Life," we speak not only of the *chaim* of 5762. We are not only written in the book of life for the year 5762. We've written ourselves into the special *sefer* of Hashem that says we will live through that terrible time. We should dance a special dance for this. We're in that book! We're there! Hashem writes down every single person. And it's there for a very special day.

It is very important that a person appreciate that he himself is *zocheh* to Heavenly mercy, either due to *zechus Avos* or his own efforts in today's world to remain loyal to the *Ribbono shel olam* and to raise himself to greater heights.

This is a very serious time, and it is a time of *simchah*. Certainly we feel the sorrow and pain of those who are suffering, but we must not be depressed, because we know what Hashem wants from us, even in this time of *middas hadin*. The Vilna Gaon had a custom that when the shofar was blown he would feel tremendous joy. Although one is trembling from Hashem's *din*, in one's heart one knows he is getting closer to Hashem. Fear does not mean depression.

Reb Simchah Zissel said people make a big mistake. They think heroes are fearless. That's not true. He said if they would not have been afraid, they wouldn't have gone to war; they would have gone to bed. They were afraid. They were afraid of losing everything. Their fear is what spurred them to fight.

Their fear inspired them to go forward. The difference between a hero and a coward is whether the fear drives one forward or it drives one back. Without fear, you can't succeed, because you get lethargic and you make mistakes.

What did Hashem do on that day (September 11)? He made us afraid. This is so clearly *gilui Shechinah*. We saw how the *Ribbono shel olam* turned a symbol of power and might into one big graveyard in one strike. Looking back, do you know what Hashem was really doing? He was answering our prayers of last Rosh HaShanah in a way He hasn't done for a long time. On Rosh HaShanah we stood, and we said to Hashem, "*U'vechein tein pachdecha* — Let people feel your fear." He said, "Fine, I'm going to answer!" A week before Rosh HaShanah 5762, He gave us cause to fear. Now He is challenging us and saying, "What are you going to do with the fear? On Rosh HaShanah you said, 'If You give us fear, we will turn it into *yiras Shamayim*. We will unite.' So now turn this fear into *yiras Shamayim*, into spirituality."

It is our spiritual values that will make us or break us. It is the spiritual values of society that will make or break society. It is spiritual values that will build *klal Yisrael*. It is only with spiritual values that we will build the future we are longing and yearning for. And Hashem has given us this chance. We have to look upon it as a gift from *Shamayim*.

Rosh HaShanah 5762 will be different from previous years. Our prayers will be much more meaningful, and we will be changed people. It doesn't happen by itself. We should ask one another, "Can I be of help to you?" When two people sit and learn, the Shechinah rests on them. What a wonderful experience and how important it is to interact with one another in order to be inspired, to remain firm, to support one another. Even if it's only two people learning, it is better than doing it alone, because each one has a different weakness, and one can support the other.

The Gemara says that the disciples of Rabbi Eliezer HaGadol asked him, "What does a person have to do to save himself from *chevlo shel Mashiach*? How do you get out of it?" He gave them a very simple answer: *"Ya'asok baTorah u'vigemilus chassadim* — He should occupy himself with Torah and *chessed.*"

This is vital now, when we all stand and tremble and don't know what will be — as Mashiach's footsteps are getting louder and louder and we don't know what kind of *chevlei Mashiach* are going to bring the final end of all our *tzaros*, when we witness the *"ra'os rabbos v'tzaros* — the many troubles and suffering." All we have to do is be involved and devote as much energy and time as we can to learning Torah and doing *chessed*. That, Hashem says, will help you overcome anything *chevlei Mashiach* will bring upon the world. With this sort of promise, can anyone say, "Is it worth it?"

The message is clear. Yes, we must be afraid, but we must not be depressed or nervous, because we have the answer. We can tell our families that we have found shelter from *chevlei Mashiach*. We have found a way to write ourselves into that book that Hashem is going to open up when everything is over, when He will say, "These are the people with whom we will start anew."

Yes, there will be tough days ahead. Let us be happy in every situation, knowing that we belong to Hashem, that we are protected by Hashem, and that He created the world for us and all the other righteous inhabitants. Soon He will bring Mashiach to mankind, and then the nations, too, will recognize that He is the Creator.

## RABBI YISROEL SIMCHA SCHORR

*ROSH YESHIVAH, OHR SOMAYACH, MONSEY, NEW YORK*

On September 11, all of *klal Yisrael* and the world trembled. Our feeling of security was crushed. Many of us grew up in a society that knows no fear, where speaking to a young child of reward and punishment, of Gehinnom, is not considered appropriate, where a parent could possibly be arrested for child abuse because he scared a child into believing in Gehinnom. But that's not the way of *klal Yisrael*.

The way of *klal Yisrael* is to request of Hashem, "*U'vechein tein pachdecha* — And so imbue us with fear of You." A Yid wants *pachad*, fear, of Hashem. HaKadosh Baruch Hu has given us a good taste of fear. He taught us many lessons that day. Now, when we daven *Shemoneh Esreh*, the words "*haKeil hagadol hagibbur v'hanora* — the great, mighty, and awesome God" will have a different meaning for us.

In this week's parashah it says, "*U'va alecha haberachah v'haklalah* — The blessing and the curse will come upon you." The Chasam Sofer asks, "Why the *klalah*, curse, with the *berachah*, blessing? It's the *klalah* that brings us to do *teshuvah*, not the *berachah*." In the bitter *galus*, he says, in a time of divine wrath, in a time when HaKadosh Baruch Hu is playing out His master plan for the end of days, if one looks carefully he sees both blessing and curse simultaneously. One sees the carnage, but at the same time he sees all the miracles and wonders — those who either escaped or were not there.

When one sees both sides of the coin at the same time, he says, "*Yemincha Hashem ne'edari bako'ach yemincha Hashem tiratz oyeiv* — Your right hand, Hashem is adorned with strength; Your right hand, Hashem, smashes the enemy." Even when there's *middas hadin*, one sees "*haKeil hagadol*," the Almighty. He sees HaKadosh Baruch Hu's *chessed*, His *hashgachah. Hatzur tamim pa'alo* — The Rock, His work is perfect." HaKadosh Baruch Hu's *pe'ulah* — and what a *pe'ulah* — it's *tamim*, perfect. No one was hit unless it was Hashem's will.

The *Midrash Tanchuma* (*Vayeilech*) says, "*Lechu*, 'Go,' is *lashon tochacha* — it is an expression of rebuke." Which *pasuk* does the Midrash bring to prove this? We would have expected it to bring the verse in *Yeshayahu* "*Lechu na v'nivavecha* — Let us go and reason together." Instead the Midrash brings a verse from *Tehillim* (46:9): "*Lechu chazu mifalos Hashem asher sam sheimos ba'aretz* — Go see the works of Hashem, Who has made the earth desolate." The prophet's rebuke, "*Lechu na v'nivavecha*," could move a person; it could give him push. But to a certain degree it is limited. The "*lechu*" should move every one of us. "*Lechu chazu*" — Go see what HaKadosh Baruch Hu did, the devastation He wrought in just a few minutes. Great, mighty buildings, towers representing strength, wealth, and advanced technology, crumbled before the eyes of thousands, if not millions. The message is "Move! Don't stop! Don't be complacent! Don't be satisfied that you shed a tear!" "*Lechu chazu* – Go see." This is an expression of rebuke. The lesson should penetrate; it should change a person. It's not just a different world from that day on – it should be a different me, a different you, and a different all of us.

The feelings we experience from what we see with our eyes is stronger than those we feel at hearing about it. "*Lo sehei shemiah gedolah mire'iyah* – Seeing has a greater impact than hearing." This is the lesson Yeshayahu teaches: "*V'shafel ram anashim v'nisgav Hashem levado bayom hahu* – The arrogance of man will be brought low, and Hashem alone will be exalted on that day." He was preparing the world – not only *klal Yisrael,* but the world created by our Creator – to recognize this and remove pride, the "*kochi v'otzem yadi,*" the feeling that things are in our control and nothing terrible can happen to us, and remember the "*v'nisgav Hashem levado.*"

Could HaKadosh Baruch Hu have given us a better preparation for Rosh HaShanah? That's the essence of Rosh HaShanah – to be able to go to shul and open a siddur or *machzor,* not just to say the words, but to make a statement, a declaration, that the purpose of creation, the purpose of mankind, of *klal Yisrael,* is to praise Hashem, as the Ramban tells us at the end of *Ha'azinu.* So go to shul and show that you are living up to what you were created for, that you deserve what you're asking for, to be written in the Book of Life.

This is the bottom line of the thirty *pesukim* that the *Anshei Knesses HaGedolah* added to the *Shemoneh Esreh* of Rosh HaShanah. Among the ten *pesukim* of the *Malchiyos* section is the verse "*U'vesorasecho kasuv leimor Shema Yisrael Hashem Elokeinu Hashem Echad* – It is written in Your Torah saying,

'Hear, Israel, Hashem is our God, Hashem is One.' " We should declare the Oneness of Hashem.

Rashi tells us in *parashas Shoftim* on the *pasuk* "*V'hayah b'karavchem el hamilchamah* – And it will be when war approaches": When you find yourselves in a situation where a war has been declared – and we are in a state of war – and *klal Yisrael* is in the midst of it (and everything revolves around *klal Yisrael*), a *kohen* says, "*Shema Yisrael....*" He arouses the *middah* of *chessed*, for if those going to war have no merit, they attain through the *kohen* the merit of saying the Shema so that Hashem will save them.

We are required to say Shema twice daily. Most of us recite it in a rush, hardly hearing what we're saying. How can those words make an impression this way? This is our sole purpose in life, to say the Shema. And if Rashi tells us that the merit of saying Shema will bring us victory over our enemies – external and internal – I would suggest that our first *kabbalah* should be to realize that taking another few seconds to concentrate on the Shema will make all the difference. We need to think about the meaning of the words and concentrate on the words as we say it. This is not just a statement, but a heartfelt acceptance of *ol malchus Shamayim*, Hashem's Kingship.

When two major religions declare war on each other, we need to know what our religion is about. We should not be satisfied with superficiality, with a casual recital of Shema. We are accepting a responsibility. Rav Ovadiah Yosef says that there are a million children in Eretz Yisrael who don't know the verse of Shema. Imagine! The first thing we can do about this is to say Shema with *kavanah*. We are one *guf*, one whole.

If we say it properly, it will be felt somewhere else. This is the focal point of the ten verses of *Malchiyos*.

In the *Zichronos* section of *Shemoneh Esreh*, the focal point is *hashgachah*. Everything we do has to be accounted for; Hashem is watching our every action, and everything is registered. This is not hard to believe in our times. In a moment you can bring up anything on a pocket-size computer. How much more so HaKadosh Baruch Hu. Where is our *cheshbon*, our soul-searching? The *hashgachah* we've seen in the last week is enough to move a person to say the verses of *Zichronos* with more feeling, with more meaning, with more *emunah*.

And what does *Shofros* teach us? The *shufrah*, beauty, of *klal Yisrael* as it once was. Our ammunition is of a different kind from the nations: "*Hakol kol Yaakov v'hayadayim yedei Esav*" — our weapon is our voice. The Gemara tells us, "Rava said: '*Ani chomah* — I am a wall' — this refers to *Knesses Yisrael*" (*Pesachim* 87). What is the protecting wall of *klal Yisrael*? *Knesses Yisrael* — that *klal Yisrael* is united as one. There is no divisiveness — not one Yid carries a grudge against another. This makes a *chomah* without breaches.

The United Nations and NATO invoked Article 5. There is an alliance, a treaty. If one of the alliance nations is hit, all are hit. This conveys a strong message. We have a responsibility. We have a bris, a treaty. If we are one, we form a protective wall. Do we feel another Yid's pain as if we were hit? It's no difference if it's this city, this *shtiebel*, this group. It's all part of *Knesses Yisrael*.

Perhaps, as an *adam gadol* mentioned, we didn't take to heart the tragedies in Eretz Yisrael. We got used to it. Another person killed, another one shot, another bomb. How many *yesomim*, how many *almanos*, have there been in one year in Eretz Yisrael? The *Eibishter* woke us up. If one is hit, we're all hit, and if we're one there are no grudges. There is love and *achdus*. We are HaKadosh Baruch Hu's army.

On Rosh HaShanah we need the power of *Knesses Yisrael.* Don't wait until *erev Yom Kippur*. Don't wait until *Tefillas Zakkah*. Now is the time. Drop the petty *sinah* and grudges. That's our *chomah*.

Chazal tell us that *klal Yisrael* has a Twin Towers — the *batei knessiyos* and *batei midrash*. Those are our towers, our protection, and they will nourish our spiritual needs. Do we use our *batei midrash*? Are they always full? Torah is our tower. Hold on to it.

There is a very important *sefer* on our shelves that needs some dusting, because we hardly open it. It's a good thing we read the haftarah on Shabbos, so we know there's a *Navi. Nach* is the *devar Hashem*, the word of Hashem, speaking to every Yid. *Nach* is our *navi*, our prophet, and it speaks to every Jew. Say the words. See what the *Eibishter* wants from us. You need *chizuk* to do this. You don't have to conquer *Nach* in one night. Just learn a few *pesukim* a day.

*Tefillah* is another tower, a power of *klal Yisrael*. How much *chizuk* we need in *tefillah*! There was a call. How many people heeded it? How many took it seriously? There is so much *chizuk*, so much *emunah*, to be gained from the *Pesukei D'Zimrah*. Daven and hear what you're saying! Take your time. Where are you running? Davening is a war. It's difficult work.

Those are our towers. To strengthen our *kabbalas ol malchus Shamayim*, our acceptance of God's Kingship, which is verbalized in Shema. And *chizuk* in Torah — in all areas of Torah — and realizing it's *Toras Hashem* and elevating our appreciation of what Torah is. Who gave it to us? Why do we have it? Why do we need it? And to learn Tanach, preferably to start with the *Nevi'im Acharonim*. The *Navi* speaks to us. We look for an answer. We look for strength. The *Navi* is our inspiration. And *tefillah*. HaKadosh Baruch Hu is so close to us. He makes himself available. He is waiting for us. "Open a small little opening," He says. The Midrash, at the end of *Ki Savo*, says that once you open that opening, don't be satisfied. That's not enough in such trying times. Keep opening it a little wider, a little wider. Every step you take, be it even a baby step, is a step forward, closer to HaKadosh Baruch Hu. With every step that we take to come closer to Him, He takes many steps toward us.

## RABBI YAAKOV SHAPIRO

*RAV OF BAIS MEDRASH OF BAYSWATER,
FAR ROCKAWAY, NEW YORK*

When suffering befalls us, we are obligated to take stock in our actions and do *teshuvah*, because, as Chazal say, "There is no suffering without sin and no pain without transgression." The Rambam writes that it is cruelty to allow suffering to happen without attributing it to our sins. It's like when a father slaps his child in the face, and the child says, "I trust my father that he must have had a reason to slap me, but I am not capable of figuring out why." The purpose of the slap is to teach a lesson, and if the kid refuses to learn, then I guess another punishment is necessary, *Rachmana litzlan.*

## Our Response: Improvement versus Change

The first, most basic response is *teshuvah*, but it has to be accompanied by ruthless objectivity. People will say in response to this, "We have to speak less *lashon hara*, respect each other more, do more *chessed*, learn more Torah." People love to look at themselves and say, "We can improve." But they do not like to say, "We have to *change.*"

There is a big difference. Improvement means you have a certain value that you are striving for, for which you have to strive harder, more, better. Of course, regardless of how hard you strive there is always room for improvement. People are willing to commit to improve, but since there's always room for improvement, the determination of whether they actually did as much as they could to improve is impossible to make.

Then there is change. Change means waking up and realizing that there are many *aveiros* that people are not trying to work on at all; they live their life accepting them as part of their lifestyle. People don't want to think about these *aveiros* because responding to them means not only some vague commitment to "try harder" but measurably and visibly making changes in their lifestyle.

That is why, if someone says, "Jews are being killed in Israel. It's because we talk *lashon hara*, we don't respect each other enough, we don't pray with enough *kavanah*," people will accept that. But if someone says, "Jews are being killed in Israel. It's because married women do not cover their hair, because people go mixed swimming, because boys and girls mix in ways they should not, because people read and watch things and log on to places they should not," people would get very offended.

Why do we accept only certain *aveiros* as capable of causing death and not others? Is it because we are reluctant to admit that our very lifestyle needs to be changed? Or that we want to accept responsibility only for something about which we can always say, "We're trying," or "There's *always* room for improvement?"

Whatever it is, our first response to tragedy is to ruthlessly audit our actions and admit to ourselves that our sins — not only *lashon hara* and disrespect for each other — are causing Jews to die all over the world. When Achan sinned by taking from the spoils of Yericho, Jews were killed, and that was one person, one sin. Everyone knows what his own sins are, and Hashem is showing us the possible consequences of them. And better he should show us in *Olam Hazeh*. At least we are getting a warning now when we can still change our ways.

## The *Churban* of Our Sins

The World Trade Center was probably the most monumental structure in the whole world. I've been in many countries, and I have never seen anything like them in terms of overwhelming hugeness. Watching it get blown away shook us up; we were shocked at the sight of something so big being obliterated like that.

The reality is, though, that what we watched this week is nothing compared to what our sins do in *Shamayim*. This world is nothing. It's a puny speck compared to the universe at large. And the universe itself is less than a puny speck compared to the *olamos ha'elyonim*, the majestic upper worlds, which are closer to Hashem. This entire universe is a joke compared to the universe upstairs.

And the damage that a few planes can do down here is nothing compared to the utter destruction that sins can wreak up there. Up there is a world that lasts forever, that is built of the goodness of our mitzvos, and that is beautiful and majestic beyond our comprehension.

When we commit a sin, it is like destroying the most majestic city in the world with an atomic bomb. All the suffering, the screaming, the destruction, the horror, and the ugliness happens in *Shamayim*. It's hard to envision what such a thing looks like, but last week's destruction of something so big and majestic that horrified and shocked so is a minuscule example of what we do to Hashem's world, to our own eternal Gan Eden world, and to this small world too, when we sin.

After one hundred and twenty years, we will live forever and ever, for millions and millions of years until eternity, in a world that we have created. Our mitzvos build towers. Our *aveiros* tear them down. The horror and the shock of seeing the WTC torn down is nothing compared to our shock and horror at seeing the towers we built with our mitzvos torn down by our own actions. We are all going to have to relive the experience of the World Trade Center destruction in the Next World. It will not be the death of others that we will experience, but our own death over and over; the pain and anguish will not be seen but intimately felt.

It won't be business offices but our own homes, built by the sweat of our brows, that we will see crashing down around us, and we will be trapped between vaporizing heat waves and jumping to a crashing death. Our deaths, our homes, our horror, our tragedy – it will all be personal and up close, taking place in the deepest part of our souls. We will see it happen, experience it, feel it in the most painful way. And we will think about those beautiful towers and the city that we built with our mitzvos and get sickened by what was and what could have been if not for the destruction taking place before our eyes.

And we will wonder at the evil of the terrorists and what kind of animals would destroy such an infinitely beautiful city created out of the stuff of mitzvos and torture such beautiful, peaceful souls created in the image of God. We will watch helplessly as the most beautiful and majestic structures go down in smoke and ashes, destroyed by suicide hijackers. We will watch and not be able to stop them, and we will wonder how Hashem could allow such beauty to be destroyed – beauty that was created by a Jewish soul – a *"chelek Elokah mima'al,"* a part of Hashem Himself. Infinite beauty and majesty.

How could Hashem allow it? We will scream out at the injustice and the evil of the perpetrators, the death and destruction they are causing. The sorrow, the horror. The lives snuffed out at their hands. And we will demand justice. We will scream to Hashem to reveal the identities of the cowardly pilots and bring the criminals to justice. And we will demand to know how such pain and horror could exist in the *Olam HaEmes.*

And Hashem will answer us. All the horror and pain that we saw until then will pale in comparison to the horror and pain and shock we will feel when we realize that we didn't grow much when we lived in the *olam hasheker*, that just as we had eyes but refused to see Hashem's justice in this world, we are still blind in the Next World, too blind to understand the justice and ways of Hashem. Because at that moment, when we scream in pain and horror at the destruction of the infinite beauty created by our mitzvos, Hashem will allow us to see the entire picture. And when see that whole picture, we will know the horror and pain of Gehinnom itself, worse than experiencing our own deaths thousands and thousands of times over and being helpless to stop it.

Because we will see that the pilots, the terrorists, the masterminds behind this destruction...are us.

# RABBI DR. AARON TWERSKI

*PROFESSOR, BROOKLYN LAW SCHOOL,*
*TORAH LECTURER AND WRITER*
*From "Reflections: The Morning After"*
*(The Jewish Observer, October 2001)*

The prophetic words of Amos came home to us yesterday. We had hardly completed sounding the shofar after *shacharis* when we heard another shofar that came with a *tekiah* and *shevarim*. The Twin Towers were hit with straight blasts and then broke apart and collapsed. And, indeed, America as a whole, and the Jewish people in particular, were filled with fear.

In a few moments it dawned on us that we are vulnerable.

Terrorists are not confined to the West Bank, Haifa, Gilo, and Jerusalem. They reached New York City and the Pentagon in Washington, D.C., and did so in a manner so horrific that words cannot describe the fear and angst. The mighty Twin Towers, a fixture in the skyline of New York, was no more. The Pentagon, the seat of the American military, was on fire. The loss of life was calculated to be in the thousands. The horrendous fear on the faces of multitudes escaping the burning inferno in lower Manhattan looms large in our memories.

The terror in not knowing for days on end whether family and friends, next-door neighbors, husbands and wives, brothers and sisters, were alive.... The panic during the day, not knowing whether the valiant (there must be some better word) Hatzalah volunteers made it out of the towers before they collapsed.... The thousands of telephone calls from parents to yeshivos and day schools wanting to know what security precautions were in place. Should we pick up our children now? Are the buildings locked? Is there police protection? Will I see my *shefele* tonight?

The revulsion to the remarks on the street that it's the fault of the Jews. The question that Dan Rather of NBC asked Shimon Peres: "What do we tell the American people when they ask, is this not due to America's support for Israel?" (Yes, of course, blame the victim, not the criminal.) The decision of CNN to run only Arafat's statement denouncing the terrorism but refusing to show the Arabs dancing in the street in Nablus. The knowledge that our existence in the American *galus* is precarious. But worse than everything is our own sense of helplessness. We throw up our hands in despair. "It is out of my control." And therein lies the great danger. As a good friend pointed out to me this morning, we have forgotten the second half of the *pasuk* in Amos: "Can evil befall a city and Hashem did not cause it to be?"

It will not do to hear the shofar, tremble...and stop there. Fear alone will bring no good unless it leads to introspection and resolve to turn our lives around. The Rambam's words in *Hilchos Ta'aniyos* are unmistakably clear:

1. It is a positive Torah command to cry out and sound trumpets on any affliction that befalls the community....

2. Such action is consistent with the ways of *teshuvah* (repentance). When troubles occur, and people respond with crying out...all will realize that their misdeeds are at the source of their misfortune...and this will inspire them to bring an end to their affliction.

3. But if there is no crying, no trumpeting, and people say that their suffering is a normal aspect of life – mere coincidence – this is a cruel reaction and encourages them to persist in their evil practices. And so, over and above this misfortune, worse will befall them, as it says in the Torah: "And if you act with me *b'keri* [with happenstance], then I too will deal with you in furious *keri*." That is, if when I bring afflictions upon you to inspire you to *teshuvah*, and you will respond by dismissing it as *keri*, coincidence, I will bring upon you the fury that such *keri* reaction warrants.

(Rambam, *Hilchos Ta'aniyos* 1:1-3)

Let the rest of the world look at bin Laden. We must look at ourselves: "*Lev yodei'a maras nafsho*" – we each know our own vulnerabilities. And in the dark of night, we know that area of weakness all too well. We just have difficulty believing that we make a difference. The holy Ba'al Shem once asked: Chazal tell us that every day a *bas kol* (Heavenly voice) emanates from Har Sinai calling, "*Shuvu banim shovavim* – Return, My wayward sons." The Ba'al Shem pondered, "What good is the *bas kol* – what purpose does it serve – if no one hears it?" And he answered his own question: Every day, every Jew has pangs of conscience and feelings of remorse. Those stirrings are initiated by the *bas kol*. But why then do we not respond to this Heavenly voice? I suspect that it is because we don't believe that God speaks to us. "What? Hashem talks to 'little old me'? You've got to be kidding! Sinful me does not warrant a private audience with Hashem."

But that is all wrong. The Holy Tzaddik of Avritch once said that one who does not believe that Hashem dwells within him, even in his state of imperfection and sin, is to be considered an apostate. If we are to combat our sense of helplessness and despair, we can only do so by turning inward. But to do so, we must believe not only in Hashem but in the divine spark that lies within us. That we count and that our actions can effect us for the better and change the course of the world. The disciple of the Ba'al Shem, the Toldos Yaakov Yosef, put it well. The three books – for tzaddikim, *beinonim,* and *reshaim* – that are opened on Rosh HaShanah are not dependent on past acts. We are asked in which book we wish to enter our names for the coming year. We must have the courage to sign the book of tzaddikim. And when we do so, the world will change. For the tzaddik commands, and the Almighty sustains his order.

# RABBI EPHRAIM WACHSMAN

*ROSH YESHIVAH, YESHIVAS MEOR YITZCHOK, MONSEY, NEW YORK*
From "Insights from the September 11th Tragedies"
(The Jewish Observer, October 2001)
Reprinted with permission

Before the advent of Mashiach, writes the Maharal in *sefer Netzach Yisrael*, there will be a period of time when everything will be reduced to rubble and dust, because the *havayah chadashah*, the creation of a new type of existence, must be built upon *bitul*, a nullification of the old one. Indeed, such external changes would call for just such an inner transformation as well.

Rabbeinu Yonah in *Yesod HaTeshuvah* quotes a *pasuk* in *Yechezkel*: "*Shuvah Yisrael mikol pesheichem....* — Throw aside all of your transgressions. *V'asu lachem lev chadash* — and create within yourselves a new heart. *V'ruach chadashah* — and a new spirit. *V'lamah samusu* — why should you perish?" Rabbeinu Yonah explains this to be a directive for a person to make himself over "*ki hayom nolad*" — as if he were born on that day. This is a level of *teshuvah* expressed in becoming a truly new person, not even recognizable to those who knew him before.

## A Transforming Event

David HaMelech also described a powerfully transforming event: "*Kol Hashem b'hadar kol Hashem b'ko'ach kol Hashem shover arazim* — The voice of Hashem is in power! The voice of Hashem is in majesty! The voice of Hashem breaks cedars!" (*Tehillim* 29:4–5). We are living through a period of unprecedented change, an experience that we never could have fathomed before. The world in general is saying that this country as we know it will never be the same again. We must respond by making internal life changes as well. Just as we will never see the same Manhattan skyline, so too must we never be the same.

We experienced a small taste of *yiras haromemus* – awe over God's might. At that moment of massive destruction, everything became *batel*, null and void. Money was not important. *Machlokes*, dispute, was not important. *Kavod*, recognition and honor, was not important. The stock market was not important. Sports was not important. Everything was "*hevel havalim bimlo muvan hamilah* – folly, in the full sense of the word." In the wake of such fear, everything becomes *batel*.

Anything we had invested with importance, anything that we had thought had meaning, crumbled to nothing.

## Of Assets and Liabilities

What is truly of value? What are our true assets and liabilities? Let us take a page from historical precedent.

When the Bolsheviks took over Russia in 1919, their first target was the intelligentsia and members of the upper classes. They searched out the doctors and the people who had accumulated wealth. People who fell into these categories quickly tore up their diplomas. They hid their money – "Nobody should know that I'm wealthy! Nobody should know I'm a person of achievement! Nobody should realize that I'm academically accomplished!" They were terrified.

By the same token, a business has its apparent assets and liabilities. Ultimately, every asset can become a liability, for when the *Yom HaDin*, the final Day of Judgment, comes, everything Hashem has given us will be potential cause for indictment: "I bestowed gifts on you to bring out My honor, to fulfill My agenda. How did you use them?"

The Chafetz Chaim gives the *mashal* (parable) of two people who were dispatched by a businessman to buy merchandise. He gave one of them a thousand rubles, while he gave the other two hundred rubles. One spent eight hundred rubles on expenses; he had two hundred left. The other one spent one hundred and had a hundred left. The one who had the two hundred left turned to the other fellow and said, "What are you going to say to the boss? You only have one hundred rubles left to purchase stock." The other fellow replied, "What are you going to say? You were given a thousand, and you spent eight hundred on yourself."

If the *Ribbono shel olam* gives someone wealth, intelligence, talent, *yichus* (pedigree), or *kavod*, these will be the basis for claims against the person. The moment his *neshamah* leaves his body, he will wish to go into hiding. I didn't have wealth. I wasn't smart. I wasn't a *meyuchas*. Don't look at me! I wasn't famous. All of his achievements will be turned on their head for his not having used them for furthering Hashem's plan. How little we understand!

A few days ago, what would your average businessman have given to be able to say he has the status of an office in the Twin Towers. "I'm not in a hole in the wall in Boro Park. Look

at my business card, look at the prestige of my address!" Today we know that it could have been a death sentence. What
do we understand? What do we believe in? Those who feel secure in their hearts and rely on the government or on this or
that agency to straighten out our current confusion and are
sure that all will be well have not learned a thing. The true
message is: There is nothing else but the *Ribbono shel olam.*
What was secure yesterday is meaningless today.

The Dubno Maggid tells about an informer whom the citizens ran out of town. He approached the governor and said, "I
need a place to live. They don't want me in town anymore."

He replied, "Fine, no problem. Go buy yourself a plot of
land in some other town and build yourself a beautiful
house."

He went from one city to the next, but no one wanted to
take him in: "We heard you're an informer." So the governor
sent him to a distant town. "All the land there belongs to me.
Choose a nice lot and build yourself a house on my account."

On the outskirts of town, he found a magnificent, open
area surrounded by towering trees – covered with snow. His
contractors came and started building foundations. Everybody who walked by smiled. *Who do they think they are, laughing at me?* As he continued building, they started chuckling,
laughing in his face. Finally, he saw that people were hysterical whenever they passed by. He asked a fellow, "Will you
please tell me what the big joke is? Am I not building correctly?"

He replied, "You fool! This piece of land is a frozen lake.
You've built your whole palace on a sheet of ice. The summer

is going to come, and it's all going to melt. Your whole structure will sink into the water!"

## Of Reality and Illusion

*"Ein tzur k'Elokeinu* — There is no rock like our God."
Chazal say, *"Ein tzayar k'Elokeinu* — there is no *artist* like the
*Ribbono shel olam."* Rabbi Shlomo Heiman, *zt"l*, commented:
An artist can paint a picture and make something look so real-
istic that you'll think it's the genuine article. The *Ribbono shel
olam* painted an entire world, and it appears to be real. Twin
Towers, they're real — *"betzuros gedolos v'ramim me'od* — fortified, immense, towering above the rest." And now we know it
was a picture, like on an Etch-a-Sketch — one shake and it all
disappears.

And we saw the face of *ra* — we saw evil, a cruelty, an *azus*, a
*rishus*, brazenness, wickedness...disdain for Yidden and for
human life. On Rosh HaShanah we are *mispallel*, *"Ki sa'avir
memsheles zadon min ha'aretz* — You will remove the brazen
ruling powers from earth." the Chafetz Chaim says that it does
not mean a particular nation. It refers to *ra*, the power of evil itself. These perpetrators of evil were without mercy, with no
understanding of what humanity is.

And yet, *sefarim hakedoshim* (sacred literature) tell us that
*klal Yisrael* is endowed with unique *kochos*, special gifts.
When *klal Yisrael* does not use these attributes properly, they
are appropriated by the forces of evil. If we do not have *mesiras
nefesh*, the requisite dedication in our service to Hashem, then
less deserving creatures — our adversaries — will assume
*mesiras nefesh* and sacrifice their lives for *ra*.... If we are lax in

*tznius* – basic modesty – then they will become the standard bearers of *tznius*. The nation that Chazal call *shtufei zima* – sunk in depravity and promiscuity – will carry the banner of *tznius* for the world. Objectionable reading material that finds its way into Jewish homes will be declared illegal in their countries.

For a period of time we lived in Yerushalayim with my wife's maternal grandfather. A Jew in his nineties, he was not feeling well on a particular afternoon, so he came into the living room in his robe. At that moment, an Arab cleaning woman had come in to "do *sponja*." She indicated that she would not enter the room because he was sitting in his robe. A few moments later I went into the living room, and I saw him crying.

I asked him, "Why are you crying?"

He couldn't get the words out of his mouth. " '*Ashamnu mikol am.*' We are worse than any other nation. They're going to instruct us about *tznius!*"

A few weeks ago the *rosh yeshivah* of Sha'arei Yosher, Rabbi Yosef Rosenblum, *shlita*, spoke specifically about improving the level of *kedushah* (sanctity) in the businesses and institutional offices maintained by Torah Jews. It constitutes a violation of *kedushas Yisrael* for a young man to become overly familiar in the way he addresses a married woman – or even a girl just out of seminary – even though it conforms to the normal course of business. A seminary graduate confided in her *menahelles* in Bais Yaakov, "The first time I came into an office and the men were friendly to me, I felt violated. Today, if they don't talk nicely to me, if they don't call me by my first name, I am insulted and hurt."

The Brisker Rav comments on the listing of objectionable objects of worship in the passage "*Vatiru es shikutzeihem v'es giluleihem eitz va'even kessef v'zahav asher imahem* — And you saw [the nations'] abominations and their detestable idols, of wood and stone, of silver and gold, that were with them" (*Devarim* 29:16). The nature of a person is that in his first encounter with the abominations of the other nations he finds them disgusting and nauseating. Then, with passage of time, he comes to view them as detestable, a matter of taste. Then they are merely wood and stone. Ultimately they are *kessef v'zahav* — silver and gold, common features of the business scene. Just the way things are in a normal environment.

Responding to the charge "We have to change" means that the criteria for what is normal and acceptable must undergo a radical change. Jewish weddings and other celebrations, pursuit of profit, quests for honor and recognition, agendas for fulfillment of desires — all of these components of a "normal agenda" must be reevaluated and in many cases must simply be reduced in scope, modified, or dropped.

## The Challenges of Conflict III...

When Rabbi Elchanan Wasserman visited London shortly before World War II, he was urged to remain in England. The people begged him, "The situation is unstable in Europe. Stay here and open a yeshivah in London."

He said, "Londoner Yidden, let me tell you what I heard from my Rebbe, the Chafetz Chaim. 'World War I was the first stage of *chevlei Mashiach*, of the War of Gog U'Magog. It was terrible, but not every Yid suffered. After thirty-five years, a second stage will take place, and Yidden are going to suffer terribly, but not all Yidden. Some will be saved.

" 'But,' the Chafetz Chaim added, 'there is going to be a third war, in which no Yid will escape *chevlei Mashiach*.' Londoner Yidden, do you think that you're going to be safe here, and I'm risking danger? No one is going to be safe from the third war."

The late *mashgiach* (of Mir and, later, Ponovezh) Rabbi Yechezkel Levenstein, *zt"l*, repeated this exchange in a public forum. Someone asked him later, "Rebbe, how do you say such terrifying things to a *tzibbur*? Are you telling people that there's going to be another Holocaust, *challilah*?"

Reb Chatzkel replied, "Nobody understood what the Chafetz Chaim meant. The Chafetz Chaim meant that the third war will rage in the minds of *klal Yisrael*, attacks on the *ruchnius* of *klal Yisrael*, the likes of which has never happened before. And no one will escape it. We will not be in control of our own thoughts.

"The Chiddushei HaRim writes on *parashas Toldos* of the War of Gog U'Magog — the ultimate, pre-messianic war — that during *ikvesa d'Meshicha* a Yid will not be able to concentrate when he says the six words '*Shema Yisrael Hashem Elokeinu Hashem Echad*.' His mind will start wandering. If you want to catch a glimpse of the emotional confusion this refers to — and the strongest indication that it is true — just take note: Everybody has just breathed a sigh of relief. 'Oh, the Chafetz Chaim didn't mean our bodies; he only meant destruction of our *neshamos*.' "

The Chofetz Chaim had predicted that there is going to be Auschwitz on our *neshamos*...and that's a relief!?

## ...and the Lines of Defense

I asked a *chaver* (friend) in Bnei Brak to please ask Rabbi Chaim Kanievsky, *shlita*, what I should say to guide and encourage people. He called me back: "Reb Chaim Kanievsky said, 'This is *chevlei Mashiach*. And the Gemara says, "*Harotzeh l'hinatzel michevlei Mashiach ya'asok b'Torah u'vigemilus chassadim* — If one wants to be spared suffering in the days before the advent of Mashiach, become involved in Torah and *gemilus chassadim*.' "

What does "*oseik b'Torah*" mean? This calls for a different type of involvement in Torah. Everybody has to descend deeper into *chochmas Hashem* — Torah with a commitment, with a *geshmak*, with joy. It means supporting Torah study with a feeling of responsibility for its success. It is unthinkable that in a generation of affluence yeshivos cannot pay the teachers of our children on time. We must see to it that this situation changes forever.

We have to love *Toras Hashem* and love every *talmid chacham* with every fiber of our being.

Rabbi Chaim Shmulevitz, *zt"l*, portrayed true involvement in Torah.

"Picture the scene if we would be told that there would be *techiyas hameisim*, the rising of the dead, for the duration of one hour. The *beis hakevaros* (cemetery) will be opening up, and all the *meisim* (deceased) will come out. In anticipation the whole town will gather outside the cemetery gates in their Shabbos best, waiting to greet their departed ancestors at the appointed hour.

"You know what will happen? The *meisim* will rise in their

*kittlech* (shrouds) and will run right past their children to spend that one hour in the *beis hamidrash*, to take out the Gemara and say, "*Amar Abayei*...." They won't be interested in anything else. All that matters is a precious hour of Torah study."

Such is being *oseik b'Torah*!

*Gemilus chassadim.* What about *nosei b'ol* – carrying your friend's burden for him, in the manner of the *Ribbono shel olam*? A Jew needs a favor. He's on your doorstep. It's not just a matter of "How do I wind up this session and be rid of him?" It's "Let me listen to him and lighten his burden."

The fellow comes through your door. He has a book of letters from doctors, that surgery is required. Read it. Think for moment of what he's going through. *Nosei b'ol.* Lend your heart to his pain and anxieties.

We hear of a fellow Jew with an illness. We take his or her name, and we mention it in our *tefillos*. Do we think for a moment of what is going on in his house? He had been a regular, healthy person who had thought it could never happen to him. And suddenly he's faced with terror. Doctors. Treatments. He looks at his family. His wife, his children. His old world does not exist anymore. Do we think about it for a moment? Are we *nosei b'ol*?

Do we feel for the parents who are going through *tza'ar gidul banim*? Who are watching their children abandon *Yiddishkeit*, and they've got a hole in their hearts as big as the hole in the Manhattan skyline? Who can't bear it anymore?

I heard of a leading member of her community who davens every Friday night as she lights her candles: "*Ribbono shel olam*, if my son doesn't do *teshuvah*, I beg You, let him die. I can't bear to see him. I can't bear the Gehinnom that he's going to have." Do we feel her anguish? Do we have a concept of what Yidden are going through?

We have to break through the walls of selfishness once and for all and become an *am echad*. There are millions of Yidden who do not know that they are Yidden. Can you imagine the *Ribbono shel olam*'s pain regarding His children? He doesn't have one child who is failing Him; He has millions such children. Where is our heart for the *Ribbono shel olam*?

As the world changes, so must we. The path to change is clearly spelled out in the protections we should seek from the suffering of *chevlei Mashiach*: involvement in Torah as though it were our primary enterprise and *gemilus chassadim* – beyond reducing the pain of others, to include feeling it with them and carrying their load.

## RABBI MOSHE MEIR WEISS

*RAV OF AGUDATH ISRAEL, STATEN ISLAND, NEW YORK*
From *"Attack on America"*
(*Country Yossi Magazine, November 2001*)
*Reprinted with permission*

September 11 is a day that will be etched in our memories forever. For many baby boomers it is the first time that they have witnessed such devastating human carnage before their very eyes. The sight of people jumping to their deaths from tops of skyscrapers, planes full of doomed people smashing into buildings, and towers of strength crumbling in minutes will haunt us for a very long time.

The feelings of fright and unreality as bulletin after bulletin broke in with consecutive attacks at the Trade Center, at the Pentagon, at the State Department, in Pennsylvania, with casualties of warlike proportions, still leave us shocked and shaken. As Americans, our feeling of security has been severely undermined. Our sense of invincibility has been shattered. *Baruch Hashem*, we have a Torah to turn to. It is our oracle for direction, as the Mishnah says in *Pirkei Avos*, "*Hafoch bah hafoch bah d'kula bah* — Turn it [the Torah] around, turn it around, for everything is contained in it." The Torah teaches us how to react when the extraordinary happens.

On the Shabbos before the series of tragedies, we heard in the weekly parashah the *tochecha*, God's warnings to our people. One can only find a strengthening of one's faith in the prophecy of the Torah when one looks at the following verses. The *pasuk* tells us, "God will bring against you a nation from afar, from the end of the earth, that will swoop at you as an eagle, a nation whose language is foreign to you. A nation brazen, showing no respect to elder statesmen nor compassion for the young" (*Devarim* 28:49). Three verses later the Torah continues, "And he will attack you at all your gates until your high towers, your most fortified ones, which you have complete faith in, will come caving down; the enemy will besiege you at many of your portals in all your lands...."

Let's bear in mind that the Twin Towers, which took seven years to build, were built to sustain a frontal attack of a 705 jumbo jet — at that time the most powerful plane in existence. How accurate the description of the *pasuk* that these were fortified towers, that we hade complete faith in their invincibility. How precise the prophecy that the attack would come swooping from the sky. How electrifying that in the previous verse the Torah tells us that these attacks would shut down produce, for we have seen that the attack shut down the American markets, the mercantile markets, and indeed brought to an unprecedented halt the transport through the country of mail, food....

While the studies of these verses that were read in shuls all over the globe just last week give us a new understanding of the power of the Torah's prophecy, this is just a start of how the Torah should help us at this trying time. More important is what it says in verse 47, where it gives a reason such tragedies might befall us. There it says, "*Tachas asher lo avadeta Hashem Elokecha b'simchah u'betuv leivav meirov kol* – Because you have not served Hashem your God with happiness and gladness of heart since you had abundance and plenty."

At first this seems very puzzling. Should the absence of joy cause such misfortune? The Kotzker Rebbe, *zy"a*, has a sharp interpretation of this verse. He reads it putting the comma in a different place and renders it as follows: "Because you did not serve Hashem your God and yet you remained happy and glad because of all your material abundance...." At a time like this, when all of us are deep in introspection, we must ask ourselves, are we happy even though our prayers are said devoid of any feelings toward Hashem? Are we glad even though we don't study much Torah? Do we have a sense of joy even though we give so little *tzedakah*? Are we carefree although our days might not have a daily dosage of visiting the sick, comforting the suffering, and helping people find *shidduchim* or jobs? The Kotzker is challenging us that sometimes Hashem gives us a powerful jolt so we reevaluate the priorities in our lives.

The simple meaning of this verse also contains a powerful message. Yes, we do the mitzvos, but do we have a joy from them, or are we hurrying through our *bentching* in order to get to the ball game? Are we glad to have gotten over *minchah* and *ma'ariv* in one shot so that we can relax with our daily papers? Do we view the shopping for our *lulav* and *esrog* and setting up our sukkahs as nuisances that need to be tended to? When we celebrate our Shabbos, is there joy in a closeness with Hashem our Creator or only the fleeting enjoyment of the cholent in the stomach and the soporific pleasures of an afternoon sleep? The *pasuk* is demanding from us a reevaluation of our attitude to the mitzvos. Let's remember the Torah's directive, "*Ivdu es Hashem b'simcha*" — that we should serve Hashem with joy.

Our prayers go out to those who are injured, to the families that have yet to hear from loved ones, and of course to those who have perished. Why good people have lost their lives in such horrific ways is beyond our understanding. The Talmud tells us in tractate *Berachos* that when Moshe Rabbeinu asked, "*Hodi'eini na es derachecha* — Inform me of your ways," why the righteous suffer, Hashem informed him that it is beyond his ability to understand. Therefore we certainly cannot expect to understand the complexities of God's ways.

We might offer, however, these words of solace, pitiful as they are, to some of the families that have suffered losses.

Sometimes it was the bravest, most courageous, and most chivalrous people who didn't make it. They stayed behind to make sure that others could survive and escape. They then died in the most honorable and cherished way, and may their memories be a pride for all of us.

Let's not wait to tell our spouse that we love him or her from a cell phone, on a doomed plane, or gasping for breath in a chamber of horrors. Let's do it at home tonight without such gruesome prompting. Let's learn from these tragic events that life is short and we never know when it can be over in a flash. Let's take care of important things in life without procrastination.

The Jewish nation collectively wants to commend the president, the governor, and the mayor for their strong leadership in the face of unprecedented horror. We would also like to thank from the bottom of our hearts the thousands of policemen, firefighters, medical practitioners, and diggers rummaging with great peril to themselves, and all of the many heroic volunteers who are out there helping to save human lives. Our prayers are with you for your safety, and may you be rewarded by God for your dedication.

It is also our hope that the American public will now be able to empathize more with the way the Israelis have been living with the fear of suicide bombings every time they enter a bus or a pizza shop or drive to work. We as Jewish Americans hope that God will show us the way, with the help of the governing authorities, to halt such activities both here and abroad.

# RABBI MOSHE WOLFSON

*MASHGIACH, YESHIVAS TORAH VODAATH,*
*RAV OF CONGREGATION EMUNAS YISRAEL, BROOKLYN, NEW YORK*
*Based on his remarks*

The main theory that has been propounded by many *talmidei chachamim* is that the *Ribbono shel olam* dealt a blow to America's *avodah zarah* — its golden calf — meaning riches, materialism, business. That theory carries considerable weight.

There is yet another theory — and this is only speculation, since no mortal man can claim to comprehend the ways of the Supreme Being: Everything the *Ribbono shel olam* creates has multiple functions and purposes. The nose, for example, is intended for breathing, yet it serves as a vehicle for smelling. The mouth, the teeth, the tongue, and the palate were created for eating, yet they also serve for speaking.

The same applies to our present situation. We are being attacked and tormented by the *Yishmaelim*, whom the Torah describes as *pere adam*, despite any appearances to the contrary. The fact that the 300 million Arabs surrounding Eretz Yisrael have not been able to achieve their primary goal, to annihilate the Jews, is proof positive of the *Ribbono shel olam*'s intervention. Yet in their attack on America, He granted these same *Yishmaelim* unrivaled success. This seems to indicate that the *Ribbono shel olam*'s objective is manifold: to show the Jews that he is protecting them, to teach us that a nation steeped in materialism cannot embody spirituality, to give America a taste of the satanic forces of the *Yishmaelim*, with which Eretz Yisrael is confronted daily, to prepare the world for what will come next – possibly (and hopefully) Mashiach – so that it might move toward spirituality, and to give the Jews an opportunity to do *teshuvah*.

The *Yishmaelim* are known for their passion for war and disdain for peace. By attacking a superpower, they demonstrated these traits very clearly. Only by promoting peace among ourselves can we hope to offset and neutralize their power.

CHAPTER NINE

# In Memoriam

*So many lost lives, so many tears. Below is just a small sampling of accounts of Jews who perished in the destruction of the Twin Towers.*

## SHIMON DOVID BIEGELEISEN (1959–2001)

*From "Victim of World Trade Center Attack," by Dr. Philip J. Kipust*
*(Boro Park Community News, December 2001)*
*Reprinted with permission*

Shimon Dovid Biegeleisen, or Shimmy as his relatives and friends affectionately called him, was the vice president of Fiduciary Trust International, with offices on the ninety-seventh floor of Two World Trade Center (south tower). After the first plane crashed into the north tower, Shimmy called home to assure his wife, Miriam, and parents that he was okay, since the plane hit the other building. He said he was going to leave the building, nevertheless. Moments later the second plane crashed into the building that Shimmy was in, filling his office with black smoke and intense heat.

Shimmy called home several times. A close friend in Hatzalah tried to advise safety procedures to help him breathe and try to escape. He tried to reach the roof, tried to break a window for air, but fire engulfed him all around. He called several times, asking his friends to promise him they would take care of Miriam and his children. He began to recite the twenty-fourth psalm in Hebrew. In the process, however, the building collapsed, and the last sound was a loud shriek.

The Biegeleisen family is well known in the Boro Park community, primarily because of their Hebrew book business, selling Hebraica and Judaica. At one time, this business was carried on from their home in Boro Park but eventually moved to larger commercial quarters on the Lower East Side of Manhattan and then to their current store at 4409 Sixteenth Avenue. Shimmy's mother (Regina Rosenmund) was one of the fortunate survivors of the Holocaust who settled in Boro Park. She and her parents, Rabbi Elkana and Dvorah Rosenmund, fortunately escaped from Austria in 1939 and came to Boro Park in 1940. She and her husband, Shlomo, had three children, Shelly, Yosef, and Shimmy. Shelly attended Shulamith, and the boys attended Yeshivas Toras Emes in their elementary-school grades.

Shimmy, a computer programmer, married Miriam Stern in 1980 and had five children.

Articles about Shimmy and the World Trade Center tragedy appeared in the *Wall Street Journal*, *The Jewish Press*, *New York Daily News*, *Hamodia*, *The New York Times*, *HaMachaneh HaChareidi*, and others. Articles and speakers related Shimmy's special qualities and unique personality. The Fiduciary Trust

Company memorial literature described him as follows:

"Shimmy Biegeleisen was one of those rare souls about whom it is said that he didn't have a bad bone in his body. Always smiling, Shimmy had a magnetic appeal that made him an instant friend to everyone he met. His genuine caring, unique devotion, and willingness to help made him beloved by the many who called him their best friend. Despite his fun-loving nature, Shimmy was an unusually intelligent, talented, and responsible individual whose abilities earned the respect of his coworkers, who appreciated his integrity and dedication. And yet, Shimmy was a deeply spiritual person, whose religious observances always took precedence and whose devotion to his Judaism was both unwavering and uncompromising. Finally, Shimmy was a family man. Beloved husband and father of five beautiful children, he took special care of his in-laws and parents and was a source of wisdom, advice, and emotional support for siblings, aunts, uncles, and cousins. He will be sorely missed."

The *Jewish Press* article included the following:

"Shimmy was everybody's best friend. His house was always open. People came in and others left, as through a revolving door. His easy laugh and outgoing personality were magnetic. Anyone with a problem or simply needing a favor knew where to turn. The words 'I can't' were not in his vocabulary. From the multitudes of people who came during the shivah there emerged countless heretofore unknown stories of charity that was given quietly, of self-sacrifice that was not publicized, of sacrifices of time and convenience that he would not permit to be told.

"Shimmy attended Yeshivas Toras Emes and later graduated from Mesivta Chaim Berlin High School, where he continued to study after graduation. His involvement in Chaim
Berlin continued on the Dinner Committee as well as journal
chairman. When his daughters were ready for school, he became the driving force in the funding of Masores Bais Yaakov
(where the memorial service was held). His involvement in so
many other institutions geared his life into a breathtaking
pace. He also carefully guarded and actively participated in
his family's tradition of Belzer Chassidus. He never missed a
Belzer function. He spent his last Rosh HaShanah in Belz in Jerusalem and already had airline tickets to be there this year as
well."

The periodical *HaMachaneh HaChareidi* article included
the following:

"He worked for almost twenty years at Fiduciary Trust at
the World Trade Center. He served as vice president of the
company, a prestigious, high position, and as chairman of his
department. His gentile coworkers, who came to pay a condo-
lence visit to the bereaved family, expressed the highest re-
gard for him. They had no previous contact with an ultra-
Orthodox Jew, and now they had nothing but endless praise
for him. He wore his yarmulke proudly at all times, and this
earned him their deepest respect. They said it was a pleasure
in today's day and age to see a person who was so obviously
proud of his religion, who always acted in a most refined and
exemplary manner, and they said what a great loss it was for
all of them."

# AVROHOM NESANEL ILOWITZ

*From "Quiet Accomplishment," by Avrohom Birnbaum*
*(Hamodia, November 2, 2001)*
*Reprinted with permission*

On the Shabbos preceding Rosh Chodesh, we recite a special *tefillah* requesting twelve things from Hashem. All of them begin with life: long life, life of peace, life of goodness.

At the end of the prayer, we ask Hashem for "*chaim shetehei banu ahavas Torah v'yiras Shamayim* – a life in which we will have love of Torah and fear of Heaven.*" This last entreaty seems to encompass all the others, for the person who has love of Torah and *yiras Shamayim* is truly the happiest and most fortunate.

Reb Avrohom Ilowitz was such a person. He personified these attributes and in his too short fifty-two years he managed to make an indelible imprint on thousands of lives. His *chessed*, devotion to Torah learning, and, even more, his supreme *mesiras nefesh* to disseminate Torah manifested themselves in the most unassuming manner, underscoring the *ahavas Torah* and *yiras Shamayim* he possessed.

On the surface, Reb Avrohom's life seemed to be that of a regular, God-fearing businessman who was dedicated to Torah. He was born a few years after World War II and grew up in Williamsburg. Ultimately he moved to Boro Park, married, raised a beautiful family, and became a successful insurance salesman.

But this is far from the complete picture of what Reb Avrohom Ilowitz was. As Rav Yechiel Kaufman, the *rav* of the

Sefardishe shul in Boro Park, said, "Reb Avrohom was the ambassador of Torah in Boro Park."

It is difficult to comprehend how this seemingly regular *ba'al habayis* was responsible for such an enormous amount of Torah learning throughout Boro Park, Yershalayim, and elsewhere and how this great man helped and supported countless individuals who had fallen on hard times. Perhaps most noteworthy was the fact that he truly never considered his accomplishments special.

"I am just doing what any Jew is supposed to do," he would say.

The unassuming servant of Hashem ascended to *Shamayim* when American Airlines Flight 11 crashed into the north tower of the World Trade Center not far from his office on the 89th floor.

Every day, rain or shine, whether he had gone to sleep early or late, Reb Avrohom's day began at 4:15 A.M., when the telephone rang and he was awakened by his longtime mentor, *rav*, and friend, HaRav Avrohom Chaim Spitzer, the *rav* of Kehal Ohr HaChaim of Boro Park.

At five he left his home to pick up the Belzer *dayan*, HaRav Shlomo Gross, who lived across the street, to bring him to shul. He then proceeded to Rav Spitzer's shul to participate in the early morning Gemara *shiur*. After learning the *blatt Gemara* and davening, Reb Avrohom was by no means finished: he would then continue to the Sefardishe shul, where he attended the *daf yomi shiur*. Only then did his day's routine begin.

But even the routine was not really routine. His days were

suffused with *chessed* and *kiddush Hashem* both among the Jews and gentiles in his workplace at MetLife's corporate offices in the World Trade Center.

Every day he would pick up his brother, Reb Shaya Ilowitz, and drop him off at his office in Manhattan, continuing on to his own office in the WTC. After his workday ended, Reb Avrohom's day was far from over. In the evening he was back at the Sefardishe shul for the evening *shiurim* that he had worked so hard to establish.

## Establishing *Shiurim*

"He was a special person with a very special *neshamah*," said Rav Kaufman with a sigh. "What he did to strengthen Torah study in Boro Park was amazing. He was not a *rav* or a *rosh yeshivah*, and yet, in his merit, many places in Boro Park have become veritable centers of Torah."

Reb Avrohom started something of a quiet revolution when it came to *limud haTorah* by being instrumental in establishing many *shiurim* for *baalebatim*, primarily in the Sefardishe shul and later in the Zichron Moshe shul in Yerushalayim. These eventually led many other shuls to follow in this way. Reb Avrohom in essence spearheaded a rejuvenation of Torah among *baalebatim* in Boro Park.

His brother, Reb Shaya, recalls how it all started.

"Back in 1985, Reb Avrohom arranged for a superb *maggid shiur* to begin a Gemara *shiur* in the Skolya *beis midrash* in Boro Park. Seven days a week, rain or shine, we learned each day in Skolya.

"Soon my brother realized that this was just not enough.

He wanted to arrange a *shiur* that was more central so that many more people could participate. After our father, who was a member of the Sefardishe shul, passed away, he recognized that here was the perfect opportunity. The ideal thing to do in our father's memory would be to found a daily *shiur* that would attract a large *tzibbur* and would immeasurably enhance the lives of countless individuals."

With his characteristic energy, he threw himself into setting up the *shiur* and ultimately more *shiurim*. He renovated the library in the shul, installed beautiful bookshelves, stacked them with hundreds of *sefarim*, and made the shul much more "learner friendly."

Reb Avrohom had a great eye for talent, and he managed to uncover several superb *maggidei shiur* and hired them to begin a *daf yomi shiur* in the shul. He paid them a handsome salary, saying, "If you want someone to be successful, you have to pay an honorable wage."

He ran advertisements in the local papers, and very soon people were flocking to the *shiurim* in the shul. Some of the most well-known *maggidei shiurim* of our time began their career by "saying the *daf*" in the Sefardishe shul.

In fact, his brother Reb Shaya noted, "On our daily trip to Manhattan, we would often listen to tapes of new *maggidei shiur*, whom he eventually used as substitutes when the regular *maggidei shiur* could not make it. Eventually many of the substitutes became regulars themselves.

"My brother simply felt very strongly that there was more to life than working 'twenty-four/six.' He threw himself into the *shiurim* and yearned for others to do the same."

Reb Avrohom had soon arranged one *shiur* in the morning and two more at night, one in Yiddish and one in English. Not only did Reb Avrohom begin the *shiurim*, subsidize, and fund them, primarily out of his own pocket, but he even attended most of the *shiurim* – at least one in the morning and one in the evening – and others when his schedule would permit.

At the *shiurim*, in his unassuming way, he would prepare coffee and tea for the many participants. He would find time in his busy schedule to bring and take home individuals who could not come to the *shiur* on their own.

People came to expect the refreshments and other amenities. The fact that he was the force behind the *shiurim* did not in any way make him feel special. On the contrary, it just made him feel more responsible toward those who had gathered.

Thanks to his indefatigable efforts, the Sefardishe shul became a veritable learning center, a shul rejuvenated and teeming with *shiurim*. This was not the end, however. When other shuls saw what *shiurim* could do and how they attracted so many Yidden who were thirsting for learning, they too began similar programs, creating new Torah centers in Boro Park. Like a stone thrown into the water, Reb Avrohom's efforts rippled throughout the community.

Reb Avrohom would approach people who had not attended a *shiur* in years and would ask them, "What are you busy with between 7 and 9 A.M. other than eating breakfast? Come to a *shiur* for just fifteen minutes. Try it. You'll like it."

Many took him up on the offer and almost always the "fifteen minutes" became a full hour and ultimately the entire *shiur*. One person who had not picked up a *sefer* for fifteen years started attending a *shiur* at the urging of Reb Avrohom. He recently made a *siyum* on the entire *Shas*!

But Reb Avrohom was not satisfied with *shiurim* morning and night. He knew that many retirees would be able to attend a *shiur* during the day, and so he set one up between noon and one-thirty. Soon the days of numerous senior citizens were invigorated by Torah.

Not every *shiur* enjoyed immediate success. One of the *shiurim* did not attract many people in the beginning, and the *maggid shiur* became somewhat discouraged.

Reb Avrohom would call him each day to encourage him, saying, "Don't worry. You'll see. Soon it will become one of the most popular *shiurim*." And this is exactly what happened.

When Reb Avrohom traveled to Eretz Yisrael on business, he noted that in Eretz Yisrael there were very few *daf yomi shiurim* in Yiddish. Not one to let such a situation continue, he immediately embarked on a search for a *maggid shiur* and founded and funded an entire host of *daf yomi shiurim* right next to the teeming Zichron Moshe *shiur* in Geulah. These *shiurim* also met with great success, and at virtually all hours of the day Torah is being learned by many due to his initiative.

Reb Avrohom showed great honor to his *maggidei shiur* and made sure to pay them on time. Before every *yom tov* he would go out and buy beautiful presents for them to express his appreciation and admiration for their work.

He was also very particular about paying them himself and not through a messenger. There was only one day when he made an exception to this rule. His family members relate that on that fateful morning of September 11, he was in a rush to go to work, and he could not find one of the *maggidei shiur*. Not wanting to push off the payment, he asked a friend, another *shiur* participant, to pay out the money.

## *Chessed* and *Tzedakah*

One would expect someone who was involved with so many charities and other aspects of community to be a loud and gregarious person. But Reb Avrohom was a quiet person who liked to do what he felt was important without people knowing about it.

Indeed, his wife said, "I had no idea he helped so many people, and I did not know about all of the mitzvos he did until the shivah, when there was a constant flow of people, each relating a story of how he helped them, strengthened them, cheered them up, and accomplished so much for Torah.

"It was not because he was trying to hide what he did," she continued. "He simply believed that what he did was unremarkable."

Few even realized that he was the one who was underwriting the *shiurim*. He was someone who was focused, dependable, and knew that a job had to be done. So he did it, without fanfare.

It was not uncommon for Reb Avrohom to pay tuition for people who could not afford it. But he preferred secrecy and shunned the limelight.

His brother once told him that he had been shown a check written out for a *tzedakah* by Reb Avrohom for a very large sum of money.

"It was one of the few times I saw my brother upset. Agitated, he said, 'I give *tzedakah* for people in need, not so that it should be announced in the streets,' " his brother recalled.

## "Ivdu Es Hashem B'Simchah"

Reb Avrohom was a cheerful person, always optimistic. He rarely, if ever, complained. To him life was simply wonderful, and because of this people loved to be in his company. He loved to hear "a good *vort*" and to repeat it to someone else. He was a "*chassidishe Yid.*" He was very close to the Lelover Rebbe, Reb Alter, *zy"a*, and after the latter's recent passing, he continued that connection with his son, the Lelover Rebbe, *shlita*. On Shabbos, he would often daven in the Lelover *shtiebel*.

Every Friday, without fail, Reb Avrohom would complete the entire *sefer Tehillim*. In general, he was a person who did not waste time.

"I never saw my father unoccupied," his daughter recalls. He always had a *sefer* or *Tehillim* in hand. His well-thumbed *sefarim* were always on the table, ready for use.

## September 11

It seems that Reb Avrohom's last day on earth was characteristic of the rest of his life. On that fateful morning an acquaintance who found himself in a precarious financial situation asked him for a loan. On the spot, Reb Avrohom took out a very large sum of cash and gave it to him.

The person, stunned by this magnanimity, exclaimed, "How will I ever be able to pay you back?"

Reb Avrohom calmed him down and said, "Don't worry,

the One Above takes care of everything and everyone."

Indeed, may Hashem take care of the beautiful family that Reb Avrohom left behind, his wife, three daughters, and sons-in-law, his two sons and grandchildren, who all follow in his ways. May his memory be blessed.

# NEIL D. LEVIN

Neil D. Levin, the executive director of the Port Authority of New York and New Jersey, landlord of the World Trade Center complex, and operator of the New York City area's three major airports, port facilities, bridges, and tunnels, died on September 11 in the collapse of the Twin Towers.

He was forty-six and lived in Manhattan. Mr. Levin was appointed to the Port Authority leadership in March by Governor George E. Pataki of New York and acting Governor Donald DiFrancesco of New Jersey, who jointly oversee the Port Authority. Previously Mr. Pataki had named Mr. Levin to the top jobs in the state Banking and Insurance Departments.

Mr. Levin's office was on the sixty-eighth floor of One World Trade Center, which was the first tower to be hit by a hijacked airplane and the second to collapse. Mr. Levin's exact location at the time of his death is not known.

Ralph Fatigate, director of the Criminal Investigations Bureau, delivered these remarks on behalf of Elizabeth McCaul, superintendent of banks, on October 11, 2001:

Dear Neil,

I'm sure you know that I have been attending funerals of

firemen on behalf of the governor. At each of these funerals I begin by telling everyone that I never spoke at a funeral before the tragedy.... I never eulogized anyone. I could not speak at my father's funeral nor my brother's.

But, indeed, we are all doing things today that we never dreamed we'd be capable of.

Neil, I want to properly eulogize you. I certainly have the words. I am sorry I cannot speak them myself.

In the eyes of many people Neil Levin was an important person. He served on the Senate Banking Committee as a staffer for Senator D'Amato. He chaired the Federal Home Loan Bank. He was a vice president at Goldman Sachs. He was a key member of Governor Pataki's team, one of his closest advisors, serving as New York's superintendent of banks, superintendent of insurance, and ultimately head of the Port Authority.

Neil Levin was more than just an important person. He was a person of grace, wit, and kindness. He was the rarest of humans — one who somehow found the time to make many of us, no matter how great, no matter how small, know that we are the most important, significant, special people on earth.

How did he do it? There are millions of answers to that question, but the simplest is this: He was present. He paid attention. He made the time.

He made the time to be a very learned person. He was up on every issue imaginable — had an informed opinion about almost any subject. He read extensively — he followed the news more carefully than probably anyone.

He made the time to make the right decisions. He cared

about issues – passionately. His moral compass was rock solid, his integrity legendary. He was the guy to ask when you weren't sure what path to take. You knew his advice would lead you in the right direction.

He made the time to leave his mark on history. His work on behalf of Holocaust survivors and heirs has forever changed the course of history. He led the fight to open up Swiss banks records on dormant accounts, pushing aside the veil of bank secrecy laws that had kept the information about the accounts from their rightful owners and heirs. He continued that fight to European insurance companies. He dreamed of a Holocaust Claims Processing Office, where survivors and heirs would find an advocate on their behalf, and he made the time to make it so.

He made the time to fill his life with love. His wife was his perfect match in so many ways. He had an instant family with two beautiful stepdaughters. He made the time to hold his friends close – and his family closer – not only his immediate family, but his mom and his brother's family, too.

He made the time for children. Every one of my children enjoyed a special relationship with him. My two older ones sought his advice when deciding to attend a high school. My younger ones played with the "toys" in his office and called him Superintendent Levin Twelve. But perhaps the best way to tell you about him is to tell you about the last time I saw him.

My five-year-old, Timmy, visited me at work that day for his special day with Mommy at her office. By mere happenstance Neil called, learned Timmy was with me, and immediately asked us to come over to the World Trade Center. As the head of the Port Authority for six months already, he had only just discovered that he had a VIP pass that would allow him to go to the observation deck without waiting on the long lines. And so we went to the top.

Neil put quarters in the telescopes, showed Timmy what he could see. We took silly pictures. It was a magical time — one of the last weeks in August when all the world seems to be on vacation and two busy New York people had time, playing hooky a little, if you will. And at the end, after he lifted Timmy high in the air and kissed him, he thanked me for letting him into our "special day."

It is much too soon to really believe that Neil Levin is gone. We promise you, Neil, that we will keep your legacy alive. We will make time to do the important things.

# DANIEL LEWIN

Cofounder and chief technology officer at Akamai Technologies Inc., a leading developer of Internet services, the thirty-one-year-old Danny Lewin died as a passenger aboard American Airlines Flight 11 when the Boeing 767, originally bound for Los Angeles from Boston, crashed into the World Trade Center. He is survived by his wife and two young sons.

In July, Lewin had been named one of the top ten people of the Enterprise Systems Power 100, a list of industry leaders chosen for their impact on the information technology landscape and for their ability to influence the industry's direction. His prowess in the field was recognized by national technology publications.

His parents, Charles and Peggy Lewin, had made aliyah to Israel in the mid-eighties. Before beginning college, he enrolled in the IDF's elite counter-terrorism force, the unit in which Yonatan Netanyahu and former Israeli Prime Minister Ehud Barak served. It was unique that a new immigrant should serve in this elite unit.

After four years' service, he enrolled in the Technion, obtained two undergraduate degrees in computer science, and worked as a researcher and project director at an IBM lab in Haifa. The Technion named him its 1995 outstanding student in computer technology. At the time of his death, he was a doctoral candidate at MIT and had planned to return to Israel.

The irony of his life, according to his friends, was that he spent four years trying to track down the murderers but ultimately succumbed to them.

## MARK ROSENBERG

An avid cyclist, Mark Rosenberg, twenty-six with dark brown hair, used to pedal from his home in Teaneck, New Jersey, over the George Washington Bridge and down to New York City's Central Park on Sunday mornings. So avid was his concern for the environment that he regularly left his car home in favor of public transportation, earning himself the moniker "Mr. Public Transportation."

A software developer for Marsh & McLennan, which occupied office space on six upper floors of Tower One, his office was on the ninety-seventh floor.

Rosenberg grew up in Fair Lawn and West Orange, New Jersey, before moving to Teaneck after his marriage three years earlier. He attended Manhattan Talmudical Academy High School and graduated from Yeshiva University.

## JEFFREY SCHREIER

J effrey Schreier's parents are Holocaust survivors. He was born with developmental disabilities after they came to America. Because he did not speak or do things other children do, his parents had no choice but to send him away to a school where he would remain for the weekdays and return home for weekends.

Eventually he made strides and developed. Eight years later he came home for good. He had learned to read and function on his own. He would travel to the city and finally found a job as a messenger. Later he was employed by Cantor Fitzgerald in the World Trade Center and advanced to mail room clerk. Schreier, forty-eight, had just celebrated his twentieth wedding anniversary when he became a victim of September 11. His parents, who lost all their relatives in the Holocaust, said this was another holocaust for them. Then, too, there were no bodies and no funerals, they said.

## AVRAHAM ZELMANOWITZ

*From "Avremel's Legacy," by Sheya Stern*
*(Country Yossi Magazine, December 2001)*
*Reprinted with permission*

T he destruction of the World Trade Center and, even more tragic, the wanton massacre of over five thousand innocents who worked there, was the sort of event that defies description. Words, no matter how many and how eloquent, simply cannot adequately convey the depth of our pain or the evil intent behind such actions. Perhaps the only way we can try to come to some sort of cognizance of just what befell us on that day is to "zoom in," to focus on stories of individuals — and then reflect that each life so cruelly terminated is one of several thousand. Every person lost had a family, friends, and loved ones, and a life story that ended horribly and abruptly on that deceptively beautiful fall morning. This is one such story.

First of all, a disclaimer. I am not an objective third-party observer of this event (but then, is any thinking, feeling person?). I was touched personally, although less directly than some, by the monstrous attack on the World Trade Center. And I was, most assuredly, touched by having known Avremel Zelmanowitz, my wife's uncle, my father-in-law's brother. Everyone who met him was affected by his thoughtfulness, the kind so subtle it easily goes unnoticed. And now we are all left with a gaping emptiness and an acute awareness of the many ways in which Uncle Avremel was important to everyone he knew.

Avremel Zelmanowitz (he's been called Abe in the secular press, but to us he was always Avremel) was a seemingly ordinary man, a youthful fifty-five years old, friendly and funny but never loud, talented in many ways but rarely the center of attention. Avremel was one of those instinctively creative individuals — beyond merely "handy" — who found a use for every odd bit of raw material around the house. Wood from an old piece of furniture was restained and reincarnated as wall shelves and a *tzedakah* box. Small pieces of lucite became a uniquely striking chess set. He was invariably the one who showed up to help install light fixtures, move furniture, pack boxes for moving. He was also the utterly devoted son who, for many years, walked over a mile every single Shabbos morning, rain or shine, to eat Shabbos lunch with his elderly father (who was *niftar* last year).

Avremel hadn't married. He shared a house with my in-laws — but he was never in any respect a "third wheel." He was an integral part of the Zelmanowitz household, indispensable for all that he gave of himself, both emotionally and practically. Looking at him, one always had a sense that here was someone who led a very full and productive life. He learned *daf yomi*. He was his brother Yankel's golfing partner. He shared all our *simchah*s and all our sorrows with equal empathy. As someone who mattered to, and was needed by, so many, Avremel was a family man in every sense. At the same time, he had his own life, his *shiurim*, his varied interests, and a job and friends to which he was characteristically devoted. It was one such friend who was to be a player in Uncle Avremel's final, magnificent act of compassion, which has already served to inspire us, even as our hearts break with our loss.

Ed Beyea was a coworker and friend of Avremel's at Empire Blue Cross. After an accident at age twenty-two that left him paralyzed from the neck down, Ed had overcome seemingly insurmountable odds to build a life and a career for himself as a computer programmer. Perhaps these two men appreciated in each other the common drive to make life meaningful and the lack of self-pity. Whatever the reason, Ed and Avremel became good friends, enjoying each other's company, while mutually respectful of the differences in their lifestyles.

On September 11, shortly after the second hijacked plane crashed into the south tower, my father-in-law, Yankel Zelmanowitz, received a call from Avremel, who said he was okay and on his way out of the building. Moments later Avremel called my mother-in-law, Chavie, at work, telling her his floor was being evacuated, but he was going to wait with his friend Ed until firemen would come to help carry Ed down the stairs.

For a quadriplegic, this was surely the most terrifying scenario imaginable: an emergency situation in which everyone around him is running for their lives, and he is left alone, literally, unable to lift a finger to help himself.

But Ed Beyea was not alone. His friend Abe was with him — Abe, whom the Irish Ed often described as a "mensch." Ed had an aide with him at all times, but having rushed down to him from the cafeteria on the forty-seventh floor at the first sign of trouble, she was overcome with smoke and couldn't breathe. Abe insisted she leave the building. He would wait with Ed. And that is what he did. His last minutes were spent standing by a friend in need.

It is unlikely that we will ever know exactly what happened to Avremel and Ed. We later read the account given by a woman who worked on the thirty-fifth floor who had made it out of the building. She had seen several people at the twenty-seventh floor "trying to help someone in a wheelchair." Ed's mother at some point received a call from Ed — Avremel had dialed for him on his cell phone — saying they were at the twenty-first floor. But the sad truth, compounding the tragedy for the victims' families, is that there is scant evidence of any sort left in the rubble of the Twin Towers. The vast majority of those who died there leave behind agonizing questions, unsaid goodbyes...and memories.

It is these, the memories, that will ultimately help us face the future without Avremel. My in-laws have received many condolences from people who worked with Avremel, saw him in shul, or had only a nodding acquaintance with him – and all of them confirmed what we already knew: that he was an unusually kind and considerate person. Typical of these was the woman who worked at Blue Cross's Albany office and essentially knew Avremel only over the phone, but, as she pointed out in her gracious letter, he never failed to ask about her young grandchild.

Memories of Uncle Avremel are invariably brightened by his wit – the sometimes corny but always inventive puns and his *gematriah*-based *divrei Torah*, which were his special way of saying *mazel tov* at every family *simchah*. And the genuine happiness that Avremel felt for other people's good fortune was rare, indeed. When my wife and I recently had our first child, Lana, Uncle Avremel visited the mother and daughter at the hospital as often as work allowed. He was as proud and excited as any grandfather. Such was his devotion to his extended family, and at the time it made me proud to be a part of it.

Avremel helping me hold up, above our heads, a ceiling fan that seemed to weigh 150 pounds, while we attached the wiring. Avremel helping me clean off the picnic table in the pouring rain, getting thoroughly soaked and laughing all the while, when a sudden summer thunderstorm brought our barbeque to an abrupt end. And finally, Avremel, a little nervous about holding a newborn, quietly going over to the carriage one day and picking up and cuddling our little Lana ever so tenderly. We were family by marriage for less than three years, but I remember thinking then, *I love this guy.* Avremel's inner light colors every memory shared by the Zelmanowitz family.

Our Uncle Avremel was a wonderful, rare sort of person; that's clear. But there is a larger story here, and it is that which motivates me to write this article.

In the first, surreal hours and days after the WTC bombing, my brothers-in-law and I were in Manhattan, going from hospital to volunteer center to hospital, along with thousands of others, showing fliers with descriptions and photos of our missing friends and relatives to anyone around, in the hope of finding any shred of information. The streets were full of news reporters from countless television stations across the country, all doing their best to give everyone a chance to get their flier shown on television; one could never tell who might see it and have some information.

At that time, strange as it now seems, we all thought it at least plausible, if not probable, that many of the missing people would turn up in emergency rooms around the city or be rescued from the wreckage in the days ahead. And so we did what we could to help find Avremel, which meant showing his picture and telling his story to as many people as we could. We always mentioned the circumstances, how he was with his friend Ed who was in a wheelchair, in the hope that someone might remember a detail like that and it would help us find them.

Days passed, and even as we struggled to adjust to the reality that was rapidly becoming apparent — that, despite the heroic, unflagging efforts on the part of all the workers, this operation was a "recovery" and not a "rescue" — we persisted in looking for information, anything that might lead us to Avremel.

To their credit, the reporters were very kind and sympathetic to everyone they interviewed. Even those jaded professionals seemed to be truly moved by the pain of their fellow citizens. But the story of our uncle, who stayed behind in the burning tower to help his invalid friend and hadn't been heard from since, seemed to touch everyone who heard it especially deeply. And something began to happen.

In his first speech to the nation following the incident, President Bush referred to "the one man who...stayed until the end at the side of his quadriplegic friend." My wife's family received calls from friends, asking if they'd heard that "the president talked about Avremel!" Reporters, recognizing the kind of inspirational story people look for in dark times like this, gave it their attention. Numerous newspapers, including *USA Today*, the *New York Post*, *The Jewish Press*, *Jewish Week*, and the *London Sun* devoted columns to it. Several network news shows interviewed my in-laws about Uncle Avremel's heroic act. Strangers began calling members of the family, saying they'd heard the story and wanting to express how touched they were at Avremel's heroism and compassion.

I'd like to think that the many people who have heard this

story are on the same wavelength as Avremel's family about this. This is not about celebrity or using the media to honor someone's memory or even about doing something nice for a good person who's gone. Anyone who sees it that way — and some cynics just might — would be missing the point completely.

The Zelmanowitz family was acutely sensitive to the perils of being perceived as part of the melodrama parade that the media normally thrives on; it's certainly one of the less admirable aspects of American culture. That's why they passed on the opportunity to appear on one of the country's best-loved talk shows, although it is widely considered one of the more tasteful examples of the genre. At the same time, we all immediately sensed that, beyond simple inspirational value of his actions — which is the ostensible reason the networks are looking for stories like this — Uncle Avremel's unhesitating loyalty to a friend constitutes a much bigger story: a major *kiddush Hashem*, at a time when we can really use one.

Ironically within the *frum* community, where there is less exposure to the secular media, people may be somewhat less aware of the story. But it is indeed a "big" story, and the reaction of good-hearted people everywhere has completely vindicated the Zelmanowitz family's decision to allow a degree of publicity to be directed at Avremel's story. My in-laws have received phone calls from Australia, England, and, of course, all over the United States, from people of widely varying backgrounds, all of whom were deeply moved by Avremel's selflessness and wanted to express condolences and prayers for such a fine human being. The value of that cannot be overstated. We are all — secular Jews, *frum* Jews, and "Yom Kippur" Jews — beneficiaries of the goodwill created when a Jew does an admirable act in public view. And we are obligated to heed the example set by such an individual.

When something like this happens, impacting on thousands of people in a myriad of ways, the Torah perspective maintains that we must examine ourselves with brutal honesty and see what we might bring away from the wreckage — what might we salvage from the ashes of the catastrophe that will leave us spiritually stronger than before? To be sure, there have already been many lectures and *mussar shmuessen* that contained generalized calls for an increase in *ma'asim tovim* and being *frummer*. I propose that we focus on something a little more specific, a little more defined than "doing good deeds."

The volunteers who comprise Hatzalah proved their bravery and dedication for the umpteenth time, making us proud, as always. But what about all of us who aren't Hatzalah members? Don't we, too, need to do something for those around us? In fact, before we get to pulling people out of burning buildings, how about making it a habit always to say "please," "thank you," and "excuse me" to store employees, customers...and everyone else? And *never* to drive — or park — in a way that inconveniences everyone behind us? How about routinely greeting strangers with a "good Shabbos" or "good morning" (or at least a friendly nod)? Naïve? Unrealistic?

Consider: In the days following the bombing, on the streets of Manhattan — hardly a spiritual or moral stronghold on most days — we personally experienced a massive outpouring of sincere kindness and generosity, the likes of which one rarely sees in a lifetime. It was one of those times when all people of all backgrounds are thrown together by a common experience. Regular people, strangers all, approached anyone they saw searching for family members and offered a snack, an expression of hope and sympathy, a human, humane connection. It was a very nice feeling – and very unfamiliar.

We have much to be proud of in our own communities. But anyone who thinks we can't use some improvement in that "special feeling" category – "We're all neighbors and friends around here, even though I don't know you" or "New in this shul? Here's an empty seat" – is living in another dimension that only looks like ours.

Undoubtedly some will call these measures petty or nitpicky. They are utterly wrong. Everyday manners, respect, and courtesy are indeed small things, but they make a big statement about what we hold important – in ourselves and in our community. For a few shining moments (nothing lasts forever), talking to a stranger, offering to help with any menial task, not just the "glamorous" rescue-site jobs, trying to contribute in any way, was the norm in this city. It would be a shame and a missed opportunity if our own communities didn't follow this particular behavioral trend. In fact, as Jews, we're supposed to be the leaders of the trend.

Many hundreds of volunteers were turned away from the rescue efforts because the city had all the general volunteers it could use and specifically needed only those with specialized skills – construction workers and medical technicians. Folks, being menschen in every way is supposed to be our specialty.

*Chessed* we are taught is a Jewish "racial trait." But it's not enough just to be born Jewish – we have to make it true.

It's important to note that Avremel Zelmanowitz did not, in a moment of heroism, give up his life to stay with a friend. He was engaged in the sort of compassionate behavior (albeit under heroic circumstances) that was routine for him when his life was taken. But, as if by a flash of lightning, his actions on that particular, fateful day were illuminated for all the world to see. Everyone who knew Avremel attests that this sort of thing – helping someone without a moment's hesitation – was typical of him. That's the beauty of it.

In *Yeshayahu* (56:4), which we read on fast days, the *Navi* tells us a message of hope and redemption – and of the obligations that come first. Addressing one who has no children, but undoubtedly speaking to all of us, Hashem assures us that "he who chooses that which I desire" will be rewarded with a legacy greater even than sons and daughters. What Hashem desires of us, we have been taught, are acts of *chessed* in every form, not just monetary.

I began this article by paying tribute to a relative I cared about deeply. If I digressed, it's only because Avremel Zelmanowitz's actions plainly have ramifications far beyond the scope of a small, intimate eulogy – if we maintain the momentum. The story of the Jew who died in the World Trade Center disaster while trying to help his invalid friend has been all over the print and broadcast media, creating a *kiddush Hashem* of impressive proportions, a virtual shofar blast heard round the world. People looked at their television screens and their newspapers, and instead of the tales of sordid human behavior that usually round out the news, they were told of a proud Orthodox Jew, a man in a yarmulke, who lost his life while engaged in an utterly selfless act of *chessed*. They have seen this, and they have been moved by it. Hopefully our communities, too, have been moved – in the right direction.

The World Trade Center catastrophe, in which many thousands of innocents were killed, is truly too large for any person to grasp, except perhaps a Holocaust survivor – and haven't they already borne more than their share of such knowledge, having long ago made the intimate acquaintance of pure evil?

For the rest of us, there is nothing but to move forward, hold on to our *bitachon* and try to emerge from this season of horror with a better perspective on what's truly important in this life. And perhaps by looking at the behavior of people in the midst of this catastrophe – the heroic and the simply humane – we can gain a greater sense of mankind's potential for greatness and strive with renewed vigor to honor their memories with our own actions.

# ANDREW ZUCKER

Andrew Zucker was a twenty-seven-year-old lawyer who grew up in North Massapequa. This past spring, just before Pesach, his wife miscarried two weeks before the due date of their daughter. He was just recovering from that loss when, in late July, he started a new job on the eighty-fifth floor of Tower Two in the World Trade Center.

Just three weeks before the attack, he circulated an e-mail

petition among his friends, stating that he had foreseen the end of the world, and forewarned that the United Nations must restrain the Taliban. "All it takes for evil to triumph is for good men to do nothing," he wrote.

On September 11, just when his wife was expecting another child, an Internet Web site was requesting help in identifying his whereabouts: "We are looking for information on Andrew Zucker. He is married to Erica (Konovitch). He is 6'1", about 300 lbs. He has brown hair and brown eyes and a 4" scar along his lower back from surgery. He works at Harris Beach, 85th floor, in 2 WTC."

A company survivor told how Zucker ran through the fire to the mail room, dragged two workers to safety, and then ran back to save more, but he himself perished.

## IGOR ZUKELMAN

Nine years ago, when Igor Zukelman was twenty years old, he came to America from the Ukraine with his parents, sister, and brother-in-law and their two children. He studied computer science at Touro College and elsewhere and mastered English in record time, enabling him to help his family and friends navigate the foreign waters of American bureaucracy. He was a mentor and a friend to his sister's children.

Although he lacked formal training in Judaism, he resolved that his marriage and the birth of his children would follow the tenets of his religion.

He obtained employment in a hotel and then at the Fiduciary Trust Company on the ninety-seventh floor of the World

Trade Center. A few months earlier this year he celebrated one of the happiest days of his life: he became a U.S. citizen. Not long afterward his sister was critically injured in a car accident, and her two children, fifteen and eleven, were killed. Zukelman traveled from his home in Queens regularly to visit her in Manhattan Hospital, often staying overnight to provide comfort and support to her and his brother-in-law. A devoted son, he went out of his way to honor his mother and father. He is survived by his parents, his wife, and his four-year-old son.

## About the author:

A resident of Brooklyn, New York, Sorah Shapiro is a journalist who writes for major secular and Jewish publications, with a kaleidoscopic background in law, advertising, psychology, education, Judaic studies, and graphic arts. Supplementing her full-time career, she employed her talents to facilitate the integration of Jewish immigrants from the former Soviet Union and has been honored for her volunteerism in medical institutions. She is a frequent speaker at women's groups in New York and adjacent states on a wide variety of Jewish and secular topics.